Life Without Cheap Sunglasses

Stephen E. Burrows

Windmill
Publishing

Thank You

When abused children are taken from their homes the experience is oftentimes as traumatic as the abuse suffered. The child is taken from agency to agency and sometimes there is no place for them to go. **The Christmas Box House** is a shelter and one-stop assessment facility for abused children—providing children a comfortable "home" following separation from their family. A home that will instill trust and hope.

Windmill Publishing thanks you for purchasing this book.
Twenty-five cents from the sale of this book will be donated to
The Christmas Box House.

THE CHRISTMAS BOX HOUSE

Windmill Publishing, Carmichael, California
Library of Congress Catalog Card Number 07-61354

ISBN 0-9659405-0-0

1. Family 2. Self Actualization/Self Help 3. Poetry

Printed in the United States of America
10 9 8 7 6 5 4 3 2 1

Cover & Book Design: Heidi's Design Works
Cover Illustration: Cary Henrie
Author Photograph: Naomi Harper

Dedication

To Janice

It was the best of days,
blue skies, with only a few billowing clouds,
that day I found you.
There was a warm and gentle,
high altitude breeze caressing the pines.
The first signs of summer had finally arrived
and a renewing of life splashed the Summit.
There at the foot of majestic peaks,
beneath jagged mountains that seemed to reach beyond our dreams,
two hearts so different, so unique became one.
You, preserved with innocence and virtue,
as lovely as all of nature painted into one frame,
and me, a soul returned
from the pit of all waywardness.
How destined our union must have been
after traveling such different paths.
Like stars in the heavens, light years apart,
coming together because of some celestial attraction.
From the beginning I have admired your virtue,
your example, your love.
I needed your spirit to energize
and nurture me.
Thank you.

Special Thanks to:

My Wife

Janice May (Williamson) Burrows

My Girls

Nichole Dalon, Jazmine Noel, Sierra Dawn,
Jordan May, Chandler Diane, and Sheridan Jean.

My Family

Earl, Carol, Rick, Keddie, Kathie, Diane, Debbie, Keith, Monte, and Thelma

Editors

Barbara Scott, Naomi Harper, Dale Barger, Evelyn Anderson

Technical Support

Steve Anderson, Leslie Harrison, Fern Smart

Endorsements

Richard Paul Evans, Jack Weyland, Kris Mackay,
The Latterday Messenger, Todd Hammond

Others

Celeste, The Magelssens, Sharon, Doug, Ron, Tracie Cheri

Table of Contents

Cheap Sunglasses

It's more than whether the glass is half empty or half full.
Our ability to see the beauty and wonder of the Gospel
depends on our willingness to look for it.
Ditch the Cheap Sunglasses.

"...one thing I know, that, whereas I was blind, now I see."
(John 9:25)

During the closing prayer, I wiped the corners of my eyes and reflected upon my testimony of the Savior, Jesus Christ. It had truly been strengthened today as I listened to the testimonies shared in this meeting. I love the gospel and what it has done for me.

Our extended family took up two or three pews in the Highland Ward that day. We had come together for the blessing of a baby and were fortunate to have heard the heartfelt testimonies shared by the members of that ward. It was obvious by the tears in the bishop's eyes, that this had been the kind of meeting he and his counselors had prayed for. Even after the time was spent, one by one the members came forward, moved by the Holy Ghost, eager to publicly thank Heavenly Father for their many blessings. Their eyes begged the bishop, "Please, just one more. I'll be quick, I promise." The bishop kindly allowed a few more people to come forward. It's never easy to close a meeting when the Spirit is so strong.

At the conclusion of the meeting we gathered up our children and picked up what looked like the remnants of a three family garage sale strewn about the chapel floor. "That was a great meeting," I said to my wife. It was no sooner than I got the words out of my mouth that I heard someone say, "I thought the bishop was never going to pull the plug on that meeting. I was tired of all that blubbering a long time ago." Shocked, I did a double take and focused more intently. This time I heard, "That was one of the worst meetings I've ever attended."

Could the two of us possibly have been in the same meeting? I have since given that subject considerable thought. How can we go to the same places, hear the same words, see the same sights, yet feel completely different about the experience? In this example, I could have easily sat through another hour of testimonies, while someone else couldn't wait to leave. One person can be having a spiritual experience and another might consider the whole thing a waste of time.

A few years ago my wife and I, along with some friends cruised among the San Juan Islands into British Columbia. We were on board a forty-four foot yacht. One night we dropped anchor in a secluded cove off the Saanich Inlet. After enjoying a comfortable night's sleep, we rowed ashore in our dinghy to visit the world famous Butchart Gardens.

In 1904, The Butchart Gardens were nothing more than a worked-out quarry on the one hundred and thirty acre estate owned by the Butchart family. They had been pioneers in the cement industry in Canada and the United States. However, the beauty of their property had suffered greatly from the extraction of raw materials used to make cement. Mrs. Butchart was unwilling to live surrounded by the scarred land left in the wake of prosperity so she took up gardening in an attempt to dress the place up a little. Well, garden she did, and dressing the place up hardly describes the result of her efforts.

The one hundred and thirty acre Butchart estate has become a family commitment to horticulture and hospitality spanning ninety-one years. Those scars of prosperity have given way to acre after acre of immaculate landscaping. Their gardens are some of the most beautifully manicured and most highly respected gardens in the world. After a time, the gardens became so popular with visitors from around the world that the family turned from cement manufacturing to full time gardening.

After my wife and I had spent several hours walking through the gardens, ooohing and ahhhing equal to all of our Fourth of Julys put together, we found ourselves in the rose garden. I had no idea there were so many varieties of roses. When I made a comment about the color of a particular rose, and how brilliant its red petals were, my wife gave me a bewildered look. "Red?" she asked, lifting her sunglasses off the bridge of her nose. She focused with real intent and her jaw dropped to its full extension. Letting out the capacity of both lungs in utter disgust, she jabbed the glasses in my direction. "Look!" she shouted.

I'm sure you have seen one of those high-speed, time-lapse films that shows a flower develop from a bud to full bloom in seconds. As I lowered the lenses of her glasses past my eyes, it was as if each petal wilted instantaneously. I could still see the beautiful shape of the flower, and the pattern of velvet petals was clear. There was still an endless sea of flowers to behold, but their true beauty, the deep, rich, and majestic colors were now drab and lifeless. There were no more delicate, vivid, or striking colors. All of them seemed to share the same dismal hue. They had only a hint of the primary colors and were dreary when compared to the true color of the flowers.

I felt sorry for my wife who had missed out on most of what we had come for. Most of the day was gone and it wasn't practical to retrace our steps and show her all she had missed. She was disappointed but instead of dwelling on what she had missed, she was thankful to have a new perspective. She was able to look forward to and enjoy the remainder of the day with a clear view and a deeper respect for her surroundings.

I was shocked. Why hadn't she noticed the lack of definition in those boring colors? Surely, if it had been me I would have tossed those cheap sunglasses into the trash right away. But then it occurred to me; she had been wearing them from the moment we left the boat. From the trail at the waters' edge, all the way to the Rose Garden. She never took them off. She had nothing with which to compare her view. It was a perspective she had grown accustomed to and comfortable with.

Each of us experiences life with different degrees of focus and vision. Unfortunately, many have grown up with a shaded view of things. Everything looks pretty good, at least normal for the 'Nineties.' Some of our brothers and sisters have been touring the gardens of life and have never had an eternal perspective to compare their life with.

In 1996, there were over 321,000 people who joined the Church of Jesus Christ of Latter-day Saints. Some of those converts may have first become interested in the restored gospel of Jesus Christ when they overheard comments made by the members of the Church in the 'Rose Gardens' of the world. They may have been intrigued by the ooohs and the ahhhs of family members, friends, or co-workers who were enjoying the blessings of gospel life. But whatever caused them to peek out from under their cheap sunglasses, the result was a deeper, richer meaning of this life we live. By doing so, they have an opportunity to gain a new understanding of the gospel with a clarity they never knew existed. After a glimpse of life, with Christ, they willingly toss their cheap sunglasses aside, and like the blind man who was healed by the Lord say, *"...one thing that I know, that, whereas I was blind, now I see." (John 9:25).*

Some children are fortunate enough to have parents who are raising them with an understanding of Christ and of His atonement. They are growing up with a bright view of their surroundings. They have a vision of the path ahead. But all too frequently, even after seeing the beauty and wonder, many of Heavenly Father's children become caught up in the ways of the world and lose their way. It doesn't happen fast. It would be too easy to recognize a drastic change in our life. It would make us uncomfortable. So instead, it happens slowly when we get into the habit of trying on a variety of shaded views; various cheap sunglasses.

A good example of trying on a pair of cheap sunglasses might be a time in your life when you got out of the habit of praying. Maybe you had been working too hard and were tired or too busy. It might have been a time when you didn't keep up with paying your tithing. Maybe you just weren't organized enough, or one month you had too many bills. Another example could be when you didn't feel your bishop was inspired to call you to a particular position, so you turned him down. There is an endless list of possible situations which cause us to reach deep into our pockets and pull out a pair of cheap sunglasses. Wearing them shields us from the light of Christ and distorts the view that was once so precious to us.

Some of us wear glasses that are only slightly tinted. We have convinced ourselves that even with them on, we can see it all. Others choose to wear those fancy glasses that automatically change tint when they come inside, (like into their home or church) and then quickly go dark again when they go back out into the world. *Let their eyes be darkened, that they see not...(Psalm 69:23) ...seeing ye shall see, and not perceive. (Acts 28:26).*

As a bishop, I was approached by a young man who complained that he could never have a normal conversation with his father. Every time they started a conversation, regardless of the subject, his dad would use it as a teaching opportunity. He would show his son the similarities between the experiences he was having and the messages of the gospel. He encouraged his son to look to the scriptures for answers. This same young man, who for a time resented his father's efforts, just returned from serving a successful mission in Albania. Now he looks back with gratitude on the lessons and principles his father took the time to teach him. His father understood the gospel, followed the Spirit, and used his understanding of the scriptures to teach his son. This father saw how the gospel applies to us everyday, in real life experiences.

It is my prayer that we can enhance our ability to see the beauty of a life with Christ. It is possible to live among a brighter array of colors. Even if you have become comfortable in the dreary scenes of everyday life, do yourself a favor and ditch the cheap sunglasses. Enjoy the gardens of the gospel.

As A Little Child

We pray that we will be able to teach our children correct principles and just about the time we think we know how to teach them, the children do the teaching.

"Therefore, whoso repenteth and cometh unto me as a little child, him will I receive, for of such is the kingdom of God..."
(3 Nephi 9:22)

It was time for the USA Swimming Association short-course championships in Sacramento, California. Swimmers twelve years of age and under were competing at an indoor sports complex, filled to capacity. The laughter of children, splashing of water, and announcements over the public address system created a deafening roar.

I was hustling between getting heat and lane assignments and video taping my daughters, when I noticed the meet had stopped. The crowd behind the starting blocks was facing the wrong way. Obviously something was wrong. I turned to the woman standing next to me and said, "I hope it's not anything serious." I was tempted to run over and see what had happened, but I could see they already had more people there than they needed.

My oldest daughter, Nichole, caught my attention from across the pool. She was waving her arms and yelling, but the echo in the sports complex was all I heard. I've been teaching her American Sign Language since she was born, and it finally paid off. She informed me that the meet had stopped because Cristina, a team-mate had fallen. Without hesitating I ran around the pool. Half way there, I met the mother of another swimmer on our team who told me it was serious.

I maneuvered through the crowd and got close enough to hear the screams of a frightened little girl. Several very kind people were trying to administer first aid and assess her injury. Her coach was holding her head still, maintaining constant eye contact and speaking soft words of comfort and encouragement to her. As I knelt down next to her I noticed her right elbow. It was terribly disfigured and appeared to be out-of-joint or badly broken, but I was relieved to see it was not a life-threatening injury. As soon as she saw me, Cristina locked onto my eyes and pleaded, "I need my mommy and my daddy." Thanks to a cellular phone, within moments she was in contact with her parents, assured that they were on their way.

Just then Cristina noticed her arm. With a look of terror she cried, "Am I going to die?" I'm sure my heart was not the only one in the crowd that was melting. I did my best to assure Cristina that she was not going to die and that everything was going to be all right. Then she looked up at me and asked, "Are they going to cut off my arm?" Almost weeping she said, "I need Jesus to be here with me."

At that point I was overcome with emotion from the sweet and innocent spirit of this precious child. I had been Cristina's bishop in the past, and we had developed a friendship that was centered around the gospel. I knew that alone I did not have the ability to comfort her.

Looking her squarely in the eyes, I asked if she had said a prayer yet. Without hesitating she asked, "Will you pray with me?" It was a request I will never forget. I was already kneeling next to her, so I bent close to her ear and offered a heart-felt plea to our Father in Heaven. I prayed that she would be strong and that the doctors would be skilled in caring for her. I prayed that her arm would be healed by her faith, and that she would be comforted by the Holy Ghost.

The second I said, "Amen", she gasped, "You forgot to pray that it won't hurt!" I apologized and bent back down to offer a second prayer, this time praying that it wouldn't hurt so much and that she would be able to endure the pain. It felt as if we were all alone, just the two of us in quiet conversation with Heavenly Father. Even though there were hundreds of people standing in a circle around us in a crowded room. I saw only a young girl who was more interested in her plea to Heavenly Father than in anything else.

Cristina was carried to the front of the building where her parents rushed her to the hospital. Because of the difficulty in moving her, I ended up in the back seat, cradling her in my arms, while her dad drove and her mom comforted her. With every little bump and turn, she let out a blood-curdling scream. She cried, "Why did this happen to me?" Her dad quietly explained that sometimes bad things happen to good people. Cristina said, "But Daddy...I haven't been so good."

I was holding a child nine years of age who had barely dried off from her baptism, and here she was saying that she hadn't been, 'so good.' It made me reflect upon my own worthiness. I was humbled to the point I felt my heart would burst. That was when Cristina looked up and said that she wanted to say her own prayer, and she closed her eyes.

She addressed her Father in Heaven, and expressed her love for Him, and for Jesus. She expressed her love for her parents, and humbly asked for forgiveness for the times when she wasn't 'so good.' With faith and confidence, she asked Him to heal her arm, and asked that it wouldn't hurt, 'so bad.' She quietly asked to have the Holy Ghost with her, to comfort her. I was touched by her humble and sincere prayer. I can testify that Heavenly Father does answer the prayers of His children, and that the answers may come faster to little children than to some of us bigger, less humble children. It wasn't long before I noticed Cristina was no longer screaming at every bump in the road. She was focused, and more in control.

Cristina's father asked me to join him as he administered to her and gave her a wonderful blessing before taking her into the hospital. He blessed her that she would recover quickly and that the doctors would be able to give her the best care possible. After the blessing, it was time to let the doctors examine her. The x-rays confirmed a terrible break just above her elbow and the attending nurse spoke casually of surgery and the possible use of pins and wires to repair the bone. There was a strong possibility of neural and/or vascular damage due to the jagged break of the bone. While Cristina was under anesthesia in surgery, the doctor was able to put the bone back together without even cutting into her arm. Our prayers had been answered, for there was only a ten percent chance that the bone could have been repaired that way.

At her follow-up appointment the doctor was so shocked by the speed at which the bone was healing, he asked for a second set of x-rays to convince himself. Cristina got her cast off two days after Christmas, only twenty-four days after the injury. Today, she is back on the team and swimming better than ever.

I believe that Cristina was administered to by angels, and that by the power of the priesthood, she was healed. I know that it was her faith in the Lord Jesus Christ, and her knowledge of our Father in Heaven that helped her through that difficult day. How grateful she should be for parents who helped her gain a strong testimony at her young age. It was a humbling experience to witness such pure faith, and to be taught by one so young. As the Savior has said,

"Therefore, whoso repenteth and cometh unto me as a little child,
him will I receive, for of such is the kingdom of God..."
(3 Nephi 9:22)

Rub A Dub Dub

It wasn't long after this 'Super Activity' that I read a general letter of policy from Salt Lake City. The letter discouraged extravagant, long distant trips for the youth. I apologize if our trip had anything to do with that decision, but based on our adventure, I can understand why.

"...pray always, that ye may be accounted worthy to escape all these things that shall come to pass, and to stand before the Son of man."
(Luke 21:36)

It was late afternoon when we dropped anchor off of Sidney Spit, a secluded little cove in the San Juan Islands. We had just cruised from Victoria, British Columbia, after two magnificent days docked in front of the Empress Hotel. We were aboard a forty-four foot yacht, and our crew consisted of seven Explorer Scouts, and three adult leaders, Brett, Coray, and myself. We had set sail four days earlier from Anacortes, Washington. Our activity would soon prove to be more than just another adventure with the scouts. We were about to learn an important lesson concerning the power of prayer.

We were lucky to have Brett as our captain. Having navigated these waters many times he knew how to avoid the maze of sand bars near Sidney Spit. Though a scenic place to spend the night, and well protected from the high winds and strong currents of the channel, it had the potential of being a dangerous place. A less experienced captain could easily run his craft aground, or wake up in the morning to find his boat sitting like a beached-whale.

After anchoring the boat for the night, Brett expressed his desire to take the dinghy across the channel to the town of Sidney for some supplies. I was getting cabin fever and always love a new adventure, so I quickly volunteered to accompany him. As we readied the dinghy for the voyage, Coray stepped out of the cabin with a desperate look on his face, and said, "You're not really planning to jump ship and leave me here alone with the scouts are you?" He had that "Can-I-go...can-I...can-I, please?" look on his face.

Don't get the wrong impression, this was an excellent group of young men. Most of them were Eagle Scouts and they were very well behaved. But as leaders, there were a few pleasures we didn't share in common with the boys. For example, after the thirteenth showing of their favorite full length movie (on video), I was ready to toss the TV and VCR into the ocean. They also had a giggle-fest over a game they called "Noodle Magic." This was a talent I hope they discovered by accident, not as a result of someone's science project at school.

The boys would gather in the galley to perform their magic. It required a bowl of cooked noodles (which was no problem, because most of them already had their Cooking Merit Badge). A young man would put a noodle in his mouth, and then cough it out his nose. The really gifted ones could hold both ends of the noodle, one hanging from his mouth, and the other dangling out of his nose. Then, the magic was to pull it back and forth and gross everyone out. To get the full effect, I guess you had to be there.

The decision was made that all three of us needed a little break, and a trip into town and back would only take an hour or so (I'm sure right about now you can hear the distant melody from Gilligan's Island.) We decided the boys would be fine. Between them, they had enough life saving and survival merit badges to sink a battle ship. Furthermore, we didn't have to worry about them going anywhere. We would have the dinghy, the water was freezing, and they wouldn't think about swimming to shore. They were trapped, *heh heh heh.*

The dinghy was comfortable and stable with only Brett and me, but when Coray stepped in, we were more like three-men-in-a-tub. The three of us were definitely all this little thing could handle. Brett turned to Coray and said, "You need to lay off the cookies." The boat sat so low in the water that Coray asked for a life jacket before he even sat down. Brett and I had been in such a hurry to make the trip before dark, we had completely forgotten about life jackets. Coray went back on the big boat and got three life jackets. He also reminded us that it was only the day before when we had to reprimanded the boys for riding around in the dinghy without life jackets.

The boys had the stereo cranked up and were dancing joyously on the flying bridge as we pulled away. They acted like they had never been left alone before. "Don't hurry back!" "Be sure to write!" Their last request was to..."Bring back some girls!" Pulling away, we tried to convince ourselves we were doing the right thing. "They'll be fine, they'll be fine."

Brett set a course for Sidney, and the three of us started what turned out to be an emotional journey. The tide was going out, and the channel looked more like a river than anything else. If you imagine the town of Sidney at 'twelve o'clock', we had to steer the dinghy North to about 'two or two-thirty,' in order to fight the current. Every once in a while we would look back in the direction of the boat. With every glance it appeared smaller and smaller against the horizon. Brett had left the boat lights on in case it started getting dark before we got back. We joked and laughed, and were having a good time. We teased each other about the killer whale we had seen earlier in the day, and how we would definitely capsize if one surfaced within a mile of us. In mid-conversation the hum of the outboard motor hesitated, just for an instant, then returned to the steady hypnotizing sound we had become accustomed to. No one said a word but we exchanged glances. Brett took a close look at the small red gas tank. He squeezed the inline bulb and then looked back to the skyline, checking the course he had set. It took a few minutes before the teasing and joking resumed, but everything seemed to be fine. We made more jokes about the incredibly strong current, and about how far into the ocean we would drift before we were rescued, *if* the motor were to break down. We teased about how cold the water was, and debated on which would kill us first, hypothermia or the sharks. Could we tread water long enough to be rescued? Suddenly, the motor hesitated again, then quickly returned to the hum. Like synchronized swimmers, we looked back to the boat, then toward Sidney our destination. The humor vanished. It wasn't funny any more. Coray and Brett systematically began to check the fuel lines, connections, and motor. We had fuel, "Everything should be fine," they said. But there was obviously something wrong. Regardless of what else was said, from then on we were intensely focused on the hum of the motor. We had to make a decision and it wasn't an easy one. We decided that town looked a little closer than the boat, but somehow we weren't convinced it was close enough. Like a game of tag; we looked at town, at each other and then back at town, the way we had come, and at town again.

The health of the motor deteriorated. It started coughing and sputtering more frequently. Luckily, after each hesitation it returned to the hum we had grown to love, even depend on. We were making progress, but it was slow. From the big boat the channel looked narrow, but now in the middle it looked enormous. Was it an illusion, or was fear distorting our perspective? The powerful current wasn't helping either. We tightened our life jackets and took an inventory of what few supplies we had. Coray had a couple of candy bars and that was it. We didn't even have an oar. We started discussing the real possibility of breaking down, and what our options would be. Could we make it to land? If so, would there be a place to have the motor looked at? I decided if we did make it across, I wasn't going to get back into the dinghy until after it was checked by a mechanic. I would get a hotel room if I had to, and Coray and Brett could pick me up in the morning. If they didn't show up by a designated time, at least I could tell the search party where to look for them.

Coughing and sputtering, the dinghy limped into Sidney. To further complicate things, the Sidney Marina was closed for remodeling and we had to go North another five minutes and ended up tying off to a Zodiac (a rubber boat) owned by the British Navy. I wanted to kiss the ground.

We didn't have any luck finding a mechanic. Everything was closed. The closest we came to finding help was at the convenience store where we picked up our supplies. On the counter was a jar, labeled, "Support the Sidney Volunteer Search and Rescue Team." If it had listed a phone number, I would have called right then to give them a head start on our rescue. We laughed in an attempt to cover up our real fears, and dropped a few coins in the jar before we left.

The more it looked like we weren't going to get someone to fix the motor, the more determined I was not to try crossing the channel again. The motor had limped to town like a dying dog and I had no desire to become fish bait.

As luck would have it, Sidney was hosting a bowling tournament and to my dismay, there wasn't a hotel vacancy in town. I was really getting nervous by then. Coray and Brett started to sound like they were willing to try the dinghy again. I've always been a positive thinker, but no matter how hard I tried, I could not picture myself in that dinghy again. We were stupid to leave the boys in the first place, and lucky to have made it this far. The idea of heading back now was truly scary. After boldly asking every person we met to help us and even attempting to bribe the British Navy, we were left with two choices. We could sleep on the beach and have the dinghy repaired in the morning, or try to cross the channel one last time. My first choice was the beach. But the more we discussed the welfare of the boys back on the boat, the more difficult the choice became. They would probably start getting worried when it got dark, and the light was already fading. If the boys tried navigating the boat into Sidney to find us, they would probably sink it. We imagined the worst, and resigned ourselves to the fact that we were responsible for those boys, and had to try and get back to them.

Pushing away from the Zodiac, Brett gave a good tug on the starter rope and the motor hummed. With somber faces visible only by the lights from town reflecting off the water, we looked in the direction of Sidney Spit. I think we were all pleading with Heavenly Father to help us survive this ridiculous voyage. The motor coughed and sputtered right away. We looked at each other, and knew what we had to do. Brett shut off the motor, we folded our arms, and there about a hundred yards from shore, we prayed together. I never served in the military. Most life-and-death-type prayers I have offered have been for the benefit of someone other than myself. But along with repenting for having been so stupid as to leave the boys alone, and having put ourselves in such a predicament, we prayed for our very lives. We prayed for our wives and children as well, and for the scouts. It was a solemn experience. I was grateful that at least I was with men who shared the same beliefs and that together, we could turn to our Father in Heaven. We all knew that our lives were in his hands, and we turned the situation and the outcome over to Him.

The next hour seemed to last forever. For a short time after the prayer, the motor seemed to improve. We started to relax in the faith and understanding that Heavenly Father had heard our prayers, but it didn't take long before the motor began to cough and spit. It stalled occasionally, but always started up again on its own. Feelings of doubt were creeping back into our minds. Brett kept saying that we were fools to be out in this little tub and that even a good motor this size wasn't a match for the current we faced. We were up a creek (or channel), literally without a paddle.

After the half way point, we could see the light high above the flying bridge. It was dim through the misty night, much like the dim hope we had of ever getting there. The motor was getting worse. The constant, reassuring hum that had been there between the coughs and sputters had given way to a rougher, grinding sound that seemed to deteriorate by the minute.

Silently we sat, our eyes fixed in the direction of the boat. As we got closer to the boat the feelings of helplessness and the fear of dying subsided. We started calculating how much further it was to the boat. Brett was a world-class swimmer, and he knew he could swim the rest of the way if it meant his life. But as horrible as the motor sounded, it looked like we were finally going to make it. We had done it. That little outboard motor really pulled through.

Brett shut the motor off and our forward momentum carried us until the bow of the dinghy gently bumped the big boat. Coray and I got out of the dinghy and tied it securely to the big boat. Brett sat motionless. "What's wrong, Brett?" I asked. "You should be celebrating. We just witnessed a miracle." Brett looked up with tears in his eyes and said, "I didn't shut the motor off. It died."

In our prayers before we made the crossing, we asked that the motor would get us back to the boat. When the motor died a few yards from the boat, it was only the forward momentum of the dinghy that took us exactly to the boat and not an inch further. Coray and I watched as Brett tried to start the motor again. Not only did it die, but the motor had completely seized up. It was impossible to even pull the rope and turn the motor over. When we returned the boat after the trip, the mechanic confirmed that the motor on the dinghy had to be replaced. We found out later what caused it. The day before, in Victoria, the boys had run the dinghy out of gas and filled it up with straight gasoline rather than gas mixed with oil. By all logic it should have seized up long before it did.

Safe and warm in the captain's quarters that night, three humbled youth leaders offered prayers of gratitude to Heavenly Father for taking such good care of them. Despite the poor choices we made, we were watched over, cared for, and taught never to underestimate the power of prayer. Heavenly Father is always there.

Impressions

"...as I have loved you...love one another."
(John 13:34)

I was thrilled to see an envelope on the kitchen counter when I arrived home. It was a letter from my friend Aslaug. I tore it open as I walked into my room and started reading about the latest events in her life and about her wonderful husband, Fred. I noticed the letter had been typed on a conventional typewriter. I was impressed with her typing skills. I never took typing in school, and learning it has been on my to-do list for eons. I have spent some wonderful times in Fred and Aslaug's home. It is the kind of place you feel comfortable, humble and warm. It is a home of love.

I could see Aslaug in my mind's eye, sitting at the typewriter with a smile on her face, getting ready to spread a little joy. She knew I would get a kick out of a letter from her and that it would put a smile on my face. I could imagine the intensity with which she must have prepared. She may have even planned writing the letter a day or two in advance. She has a meticulous and systematic way of doing things, getting everything ready and in its proper order. First, she would take the cover off the old typewriter and position her chair just right. Then she would select a suitable paper. She'd take her time to get the paper started straight, as she rolled it into the old machine. Just the right margin and not too near the top of the paper, then she would begin, "To my dear friend Steve."

Aslaug is a mature and thoughtful woman, who was born in Norway. She is a kind woman with a wonderful sense of humor. She wrote, "Fred got a new radio. We're going on a trip soon." And, "Guess who I bumped into this week?" Once again I thought of her diligent effort to get everything just right. You see, English is not her native language, but her fourth. I'm sure she made a special effort not to misspell words. As I turned the page I noticed something peculiar about the letter. It had become increasingly more difficult to read. As I read, my heart was filled with joy. I was grinning from ear to ear when I noticed the words were getting lighter and lighter until eventually, they completely disappeared. It was obvious that the ribbon on the old typewriter had finally given out. After I explained what a perfectionist Aslaug is, you might agree that she probably checked the ribbon before she started. She would have made sure the ribbon wasn't twisted or at the end of the spool. But even after all her preparation, her painstaking effort to get everything just right, who would have guessed the ribbon would run out? Meanwhile, Aslaug, thoughtfully focused on the task at hand, maybe even smiling and laughing at her own silly comments, continued to forge ahead with her letter. She was unaware that the thoughts and words she was expressing, failed to appear on the paper. You see, my friend Aslaug is deaf and blind. She had no way of knowing that the old typewriter wasn't doing its part in making this letter a masterpiece.

I had read just enough of her letter to whet my appetite, and I wasn't willing to miss out on the rest of her message. Aslaug is a strong willed person, and either because of her Norwegian blood, or the many obstacles she has faced and overcome in her life, she does not take anything lightly. She types with deliberate and crisp strokes. I found that if I held the letter up to the window and if the light was just right, I could still read it. She had made a strong impression on the paper with her confident stroke of the keys.

As we strive to share the important message of the gospel, even our personal testimonies of the Savior; as we strive to love one another, bear one another's burdens, and to lift up the hands that hang down; as we try to spread a little joy by putting a smile on the face of a friend; if our heart is in the right place, the message will always get through, regardless of our weaknesses and imperfections. We just have to make a good impression.

When I finished the Interpreter Training Program, I spent about two years interpreting for the deaf and blind. Without question, my deaf-blind friends are the greatest inspiration to me.
This story is for: Aslaug, Dee, Jackie, Remo and many others.

The Morning Wakes

I try to remember to give thanks every morning,
for the new day.

"[It is of] the Lord's mercies that we are not consumed,
because his compassions fail not."

"[They are] new every morning: great [is] thy faithfulness."
(Lamentations 3:22-23)

The Morning Wakes

Rolling over, through blurry eyes I strained to see the day.
Past the shutters, beyond the window pane,
the treetops were silhouetted by a pale blue sky.
Rubbing away the sleep and focusing, the leaves began to take shape.
The night was so quick, I didn't toss or turn
and I don’t remember dreaming.
It was as if everything had stopped, held in check,
a pause while the stars passed by.
Even the view outside my window had a quiet, passive feel.
With each passing moment my curiosity grew. It was an eerie feeling.
Like oil on canvas, the view from my bed,
though gorgeous didn't seem real.
Could it really be dead calm, even so, where were the birds or a
passing cloud?
After what seemed forever,
the highest leaves gave way to flutter
at a wisp of a breeze.
I could live with that. It was truly a new day
I hadn't woken up in a void of activity.
Not that I’m so wrapped up in the hustle,

so driven that a quiet still morning is a threat to me.
I was thinking of this and thinking of that,
when a tiny bird dove past my window.
I heard a car start. Someone's sprinkler kicked on,
and my daughter turned on her shower.
That was more like it. Action,
movement, the business of life,
the business of living.
Some days meet us head on with trials,
with situations that are difficult to endure.
Other times we are faced with the strife of others,
often when there is little we can do to help.
But this is the life we live. It is our opportunity,
for our benefit.
I look forward to the rooster that crows
outside my window every morning.
Even if I've threatened to kill it, it's only talk.
I'm actually very thankful to have ears to hear it.
I'm thankful to have eyes that see the stillness,
and for a heart that feels a love for life...
...as the morning wakes.

A Recovery Of Souls

For eight years I managed service stations in Colorado.
Twenty-four hour towing provides some interesting experiences
in the Rocky Mountains.
Long after the injured had been taken to the hospital,
many times I would pull up to the scene of an accident
and find a Highway Patrolman staring over the edge of a steep drop-off.
Often times he would shake his head and say,
'I don't know how you'll ever get that one.'
Looking down at the car, trapped between rocks,
behind trees, and overturned,
I could understand the feelings of the officer.
But for me, recoveries were a rewarding challenge.
I loved it.

"What man of you, having an hundred sheep, if he lose one of them,
doth not leave the ninety and nine in the wilderness,
and go after that which is lost, until he find it?"
(Luke 15:4)

"Are you available for a recovery?" the dispatcher asked. It wasn't an unusual request since I had been towing for the Colorado State Patrol for almost eight years. I was busy that day, but there was a strange urgency in the dispatcher's voice. I looked out the window to make sure one of my mechanics hadn't taken the wrecker on a parts run. "Yes, I can do it," I answered. The dispatcher then rushed through the details, "I have a recovery at mile marker 116, on Highway 9. And please hurry! The car is hanging over a cliff and the people are still in it."

I'm not even sure I hung up the phone. I was in my truck and miles down the road before I radioed the shop to tell them where I had gone. I have never been accused of being a slow driver, even on snow-packed roads, but that day my adrenaline was pumping. The State Patrol needed me. They had told me to hurry and that there were lives in danger. I reached over and turned on the emergency beacons that were mounted on top of my wrecker. They were only supposed to be used by the State Patrol, Sheriff's vehicles, fire trucks and ambulances, but I was going all out. The situation was critical and time was running out. There was a rescue in progress and people were counting on me.

When I was a baby, the car my mom was driving slid off an icy highway just outside Aspen, Colorado. The only thing that kept our family from crashing into the Roaring Fork River was an aspen tree. As I thought of another family stranded in a similar situation, I prayed that they would be able to hang on until I got there. I pushed harder on the gas.

As I approached the accident scene, I recognized it as a dangerous curve where many others had lost control and died. Traffic was backed up for miles in both directions. It was a mess and flashing lights were everywhere. There were two huge fire trucks, patrol cars, search and rescue teams, ambulances, and dozens of skilled professionals who were trained for this very situation. Before I slowed down a fireman who was standing on top of his truck, motioned for me to back in between the two fire trucks.

It was time for me to go to work. I was on auto-pilot and had done this a thousand times before. Every call I had ever responded to had prepared me for this particular one.

I backed in between the two fire trucks, slammed on my emergency brake and pushed in the clutch. I pulled the power-take-off into gear and flew out the door all in one movement. I disengaged the clutch on the left wench, lifted the hook from the sling, and ran toward the cliff, ripping cable off the spool. With both arms reaching in front of me, I passed the hook to the search and rescue team member. He was already hooked into a safety rope when he grabbed the hook and disappeared over the edge. I didn't even look for the car. I ran back to the wrecker and hefted one of the heavy chalk blocks off the back of the truck. I slammed the wedge behind the big dual wheels of my truck and secured the chain from the chalk block to the truck. Then I repeated the whole process again on the right side of the truck.

Chalk blocks are an important tool and protection in a recovery. When the wench pulls hard, and the cables are strong, something will give. If the highway is covered with ice, as it was that day, and if the load is heavy, instead of pulling the car up the cliff, the wench could pull the wrecker toward the cliff. However, with the chalk blocks securely in place, the wrecker pulls its own weight against the chalks, which in turn dig their sharp teeth deeper into the ice or asphalt. Chalks will hold the tow truck firm. Then, when the wench pulls hard, all progress will be in the direction of safety.

After setting the second chalk block, I disengaged the clutch for the wench, pulled out on the throttle control increasing the r.p.m.s of the engine, and took up the slack as fast as I could. It went like clockwork. By the time the rescue worker had attached my cable to the vehicle, I had my chalks dug in and my cable taunt. That car wasn't going anywhere. I was having fun and it felt good to be involved in something as important as a rescue.

I walked over to the edge of the cliff and for the first time I saw the car. It was upside down and teetering against an evergreen tree that had been struggling to grow on the steep slope. The rescue workers had been afraid to touch the car much less try to get the occupants out. They were afraid of upsetting the delicate balance and causing the whole kit and kabutal to end up in the swift currents and icy waters of the Blue River. I sat down, dangled my feet over the edge and watched as the drama unfolded.

One of the rescue workers made his way under the car and yelled, "Okay, Elaine, we're ready to get you out of there now." I turned to the firemen next to me and asked who was in the car. "Just one older lady named Elaine," he said. I looked back to see if I could recognize the car, but the only parts I could see were the drive line and four tires. Summit County isn't a very big community and I only knew one Elaine. I yelled down and asked if it was Elaine Furman in the car. He said that it was. My heart skipped a beat. I was her home teacher.

I didn't ask for permission, I grabbed the safety rope and shinnied down as close to the car as I could get. I yelled to Elaine and told her I was there. I told her not to worry because I had secured the car and that everything was going to be all right.

With the car secure, the rescue workers jumped in and did their jobs. It didn't take long before they managed to get Elaine onto a litter and pull her out through the broken back window. I joined the others, and together we pulled the litter up the cliff to safety. Just before they put Elaine into the ambulance, she motioned for me to come near. She held my hand and quietly told me that her day had started out like any other. She had gone down the valley to pick up some grain for her horses, and before she knew it, her life was literally turned upside down. She told me that while injured and lying on the inside roof of her car, listening to the sound of the river rushing below her, she had been comforted knowing there was someone that she knew helping with her rescue.

Several years later I received a call from a different kind of dispatcher. It was my High Priest Group Leader. When he called, he might as well have asked, "Are you available for a recovery?" He wanted to know if I would be willing to add another family to my Home Teaching route. I was busy at the time with my own family and other callings, but I told him I could do it.

The assignment was to visit a family in our ward that hadn't been active for almost six years. From the first time I knocked on their front door, I have been welcome in their home. They have treated me like part of their family. At the end of my first visit they walked me to my car as if they didn't want me to leave. They were knowledgeable in the gospel and had been members of the Church longer than I had been. I think they even knew more people in the stake than I did. Both the husband and wife had served in several different callings and would have been a wonderful asset to our ward. At the end my visit they were happy to have a closing prayer and to tell you the truth, they didn't seem any different than any other member of our ward. I made sure before I left to let them know that their ward family loved them. I invited them to start attending church again and told them what time Sacrament Meeting was held. I also let them know that we needed them.

I couldn't wait to call my High Priest Group Leader and tell him about my visit. I told him that the family I was Home Teaching would probably be in church on Sunday. I told him they knew the gospel was true, and that they were great. There was really no good reason for them to stay away. "I promise they'll come!" I said. I told everyone. But they didn't come.

Every month I visited them. We talked about our families and our jobs, and I even gave a lesson now and then. But they didn't come. We became good friends, but they didn't come. I was always welcome in their home, but they didn't come.

Then one night I went to visit them and the Elders Quorum Presidency were already there sitting on the couch. They had come to visit and get better acquainted with the family. Another night the bishop and one of his counselors dropped by. Later I found that the Relief Society visiting teachers had been showing their love and concern by calling and visiting regularly. At Christmas time the young men and young women from our ward stood at the family's door bearing plates of cookies, and sang Christmas carols for them.

One night to my surprise, they called me! They had been asked by the Ward Mission Leader if they would provide a meal for the full-time missionaries in their home. They willingly accepted the assignment and when they called, they had just finished the meal. They were excited about it and knew I would be happy to know. They told me it was great, but they still didn't come to church.

After about two years of promising my bishop that this good family was going to come to church, I pulled into their driveway with a new plan. I had already shared my testimony with them, and they knew they should be going to church. More than once they told me not to be surprised when they did, but still they never came. I walked into the house, gave my lesson, and before the closing prayer I asked them to do me a favor. I confessed to them that I had been promising the bishop and everybody else that they were going to be in the pews. I simply asked them to make an honest person out of me.

This couple are once again active participants in the restored gospel of Jesus Christ. They are both serving in callings in our ward. Through a renewed commitment and involvement in the Church, the blessings of the gospel are becoming more and more evident in their lives. They are preparing to go back to the temple and partake of the special spirit and blessings of temple attendance.

I didn't bring this family back into activity any more than I saved Elaine Furman's life. In both recoveries, I merely established a connection, a connection of safety, a connection of concern, a connection of love. The real recovery in both stories was made possible by many talented individuals, people whose experiences had prepared them to do their part in the recovery of souls.

Each of us have received an urgent call from the Lord's dispatcher. President Hinkley wants to know if you're available for a recovery. If it helps you understand the urgency of the call, picture the emergency beacons flashing. Get your adrenaline pumping. There is no shortage of talented individuals standing by willing to help. Sometimes we're too afraid of upsetting the delicate balance of someone who is teetering above the treacherous waters of transgression. As visiting teachers and home teachers we must establish a safe connection between our less active brothers and sisters and the bishop–a connection of trust between them and the Church–a connection of love between them and the Savior. If we can do that, the ward rescue workers, like spiritual paramedics, fireman, ambulance drivers, doctors and nurses of the gospel can do their jobs. Each and every member of the ward family can assist in lifting precious souls back into the arms of peace, into the arms of joy, into the loving arms of the Savior.

Back To The Fold

Search for the one.

*"If a man say, I love God, and hateth his brother, he is a liar:
for he that loveth not his brother whom he hath seen,
how can he love God whom he hath not seen?"
(1 John 4:20)*

Back To The Fold

We have brothers and sister, fathers and mothers,
we have neighbors, there are people we love;
Who for all their own reasons and countless others,
have strayed from our Father above.
Not always from a single event in their life,
it may have started with sickness or pain;
But as the habit develops, one of heart ache and strife,
whatever the cause, the result is the same.
While outwardly they may appear to be fine,
there is something so important that's missing;
And if that void is left open, for an extended period of time,
they could loose out on their most precious blessing.
Oft times when church attendance is set to the side,
other principles are soon quick to follow;
And when transgression sets in, there's so much to hide,
repentance looks like a lot to swallow.
Then comes from a Prophet, his plea throughout the land,
begging all to come back to the fold;
It is our charge to be standing with an outstretched hand,
to welcome them back, young and old.
We're to follow the Savior, to search for the one,
they are all very precious in his sight;
Even in our own families, the search must begin,
and bring each one back into the light.
If we're truly a family of one heart and one mind,
we'll dig down and commit to the task;
We'll be patient, and diligent, long suffering and kind,
and do all that the Savior might ask.
When all the dust settles, and we look back on this day,
if there be but one child added back to the fold;
How great shall be your joy, and this much I can say,
it will be better than riches and gold.

Finish The Course

When I hear people say, 'I can't wait until my children are raised, then I can...'
Or,
'When I can afford it, I'm going to...'

Patience is a good thing, but I don't think happiness is something that we have to wait for. It's found in the process of living.

"...that I might finish my course with joy,
and the ministry, which I have received of the Lord Jesus,
to testify the gospel of the grace of God."
(Acts 20:24)

March 16, 1996 was a chilly day in Woodland, California. I was timing in lane three at a swim meet and the next heat was about to begin. The starter called the girls to, "Step up." A few of the girls knelt down by the edge of the pool to splash, (a ritualistic mixture of getting used to the water temperature and intimidating their opponent.) The girls climbed onto their starting blocks. The starter's voice echoed across the complex, "Girls, your feet must be an equal distance from the front of the block. Come down on my count. This is a 200 meter individual medley." The girls were focused when the starter said, "Swimmers take your mark." At once, the strobe flashed and the tone sounded. The girls shot from their blocks like gazelles, diving for the opposite end of the pool. As the first girls surfaced and started the butterfly leg of the race, I caught a glimpse of the girl in lane one, half dive, half jump into the pool. Before I turned my head to see who she was, my mind wandered to when my daughters swam on a recreational team. I could still see the little kids age eight and under hitting the water with enthusiasm, but with very little style. Children are so precious.

My daydream was interrupted by a man who was timing in lane two. He was laughing out loud and pointing his finger at the swimmer in lane one. In a sarcastic tone he mocked, "Now THAT is going to be a long 200!"

I looked to the pool and there in lane one was a young girl struggling to swim the butterfly. She appeared to have a physical disability and was having trouble getting her arms all the way out of the water. The girl's difficulty reminded me of my niece, Tracie. She was born three months premature and spent the first three and a half months of her life in an incubator. She endured open heart surgery as a three pound 'preemie,' and dropped to a dangerous 2.2 pounds before she started the long process of recovery. As a family we are grateful for the mere fact that she is alive today, twenty-three years later, and for her sweet loving spirit. Regardless of her disabilities, she is an important part of our family. And if Tracie were able to swim one lap in this pool, I would be as proud of her as if she had won a Gold Medal in the Olympics.

That day in Woodland I was saddened by the comment of the man in lane two and struggled to control myself. I wanted to march over and give him a serious tongue-lashing, but I was calmed by reflecting on the words of the greatest of all teachers, *"...Father, forgive them; for they know not what they do..."(Luke 23:34)* While the Savior of the world hung, nailed to the cross, scourged and bleeding, he prayed for those who stoned and mocked him, forgiving those who spat upon him. The question was, could I follow his example and overlook the ignorance of the man in lane two?

Suddenly I felt embarrassed for him and hoped the cheering crowd had prevented most people from hearing his insensitive remark. I turned and scanned the crowd behind the blocks. Swimmers on deck were stretching their muscles, and waiting for upcoming events. Teammates were shouting in support of their friends. There were grandmothers holding bottles of sunscreen, and dads armed with video cameras. But there behind lane one, alone in the crowd, stood a different kind of competitor. She wasn't paying attention to the hustle and bustle of the crowd. Dotty McCarthy, the mother who had carried, delivered, nurtured, and whole heartedly supported the young lady swimming in lane one. Supporting her not only in swimming, but in every aspect of her life. She was intense as she stared at the progress of her swimmer. She was tan and obviously no stranger to the deck of a pool. With a towel in hand to warm the victor, her eyes were fixed on the pool. She seemed so consciously focused, I don't think she was affected at all by her surroundings.

Dotty went into labor almost four months early with her twin girls. The doctors were unsuccessful in stopping her labor and gave Dotty and her husband Sean, little or no hope that the babies would survive. On March 21, 1984 at 1:46 in the afternoon, Kelly McCarthy became the big sister by a full two minutes. She weighed in at one pound eight ounces and Erin was delivered breach, weighing one pound ten ounces. They were so tiny Sean's wedding ring could fit over the entire length of their arms and legs.

After the girls were born, Dotty caught only a glimpse of Erin and a mere touch of Kelly's face, before the girls were rushed away by nurses and doctors, who for the next three months would poke and prod at them from every angle. The McCarthy twins were to be subjected to every test and procedure modern science could dish out, including open heart surgery which was scheduled two weeks after they were born. There were many ups and downs for the twins during those first few months, but there was only one question that mattered: would their daughters live? The doctors refused to make any commitments as to any possible future for the girls. They claimed the babies were too small to survive and that they were suffering from too many serious complications. The doctors counseled Dotty and Sean not to get too attached to them, because they probably wouldn't make it.

Dotty and Sean lived eighty miles from Tucson Medical Center's, High Risk Nursery where the twins lived for three months. They can still remember the difficulties they went through, such as the phone call in the middle of the night when doctors told them Erin suffered a brain bleed, and would probably be dead before they could get to the hospital. Erin didn't die. They remember the spinal taps that were done on the girls to rule out meningitis when one of them was burning up with a fever. Both girls were diagnosed with Cerebral Palsy but so far, only the right side of Kelly's body has been affected by it. With each day the babies survived and each physical battle they overcame, no matter how hard the nurses and doctors tried to avoid getting attached, they fell in love with the McCarthy twins. Because of their Irish names, the hospital staff and the Tucson media started calling the twins, "The Fighting Irish."

Having been delivered at twenty-five weeks, the girls lungs were not fully developed and they required months of oxygen therapy, and the use of a respirator. There are serious risks involved with the use of oxygen. If the babies didn't get enough, they would run the risk of brain damage. On the other hand, if they received too much oxygen it would damage their retinas. The doctors reported that both girls' eyes were fine, until the day they were to come home. That was when Dotty and Sean were told Kelly was almost completely blind. Blind and stricken with Cerebral Palsy, Kelly McCarthy has had to fight to succeed in every aspect of her life.

Back at the pool in Woodland, all but one of the swimmers had finished the race and were scurrying off to see their coaches for a post race critique. But there in lane one was Kelly Mccarthy, still swimming. Her race was not over. She still had another two laps of free-style to go. On the clock, the hundredths of a second seemed to be a blur in the passing of time, and yet Kelly maintained a constant, one stroke at a time determination to finish. Her version of the Australian Crawl isn't the same as her teammates. She has a style all her own. Though she is legally blind, if she lifts her head up occasionally, and in the right light, she has a chance of seeing the wall before she gets to it. She may not have the most graceful or smooth stroke, but she makes every stroke and kick count.

As she made the final turn and started her last lap, most people at the meet were unaware that the race was still in progress. People were standing in line at the snack bar waiting to buy blow-pops and nachos. Others were under their sunshades. Some kids were playing cards, and some of the adults were relaxing with their novels. But there were a few people lucky enough to be at the South end of the pool, a few people close enough to Kelly McCarthy to witness a real champion set a personal record.

Often while watching my daughters at the start of a race, I find myself pushing up onto my toes. It's an unconscious reaction and somehow I feel that it gives them an extra boost on the start. Today as Kelly was making her way to the finish, I was kicking and pulling with all my heart. I wanted to share my strength with her. I wanted her to win.

I looked back at the man who was timing in lane two. I wondered if he felt like a fool for having made such an insensitive remark earlier. Each of us may recall a time when in an attempt to be cute or funny, we have said something that we later realized was wrong. People have a tendency to judge others by first impressions, by stereotypes, and according to their prejudices. As Kelly took the last few strokes to the wall, I was as proud as if she were one of my own daughters. We were not in Atlanta at the Olympic Games, but she deserved to stand on a podium and to hear the National Anthem. I would have loved to be the one who placed a gold medal around her neck. And if I had been wearing a hat, I would have thrown it into the air for the real winner, Kelly McCarthy.

"...Look not on his countenance, or on the height of his stature;
...[for the Lord seeth] not as man seeth; for man looketh on the outward appearance, but the Lord looketh on the heart."
(1 Samuel 16:7)

Jump!

During my younger days I didn't always jump when I was asked to. As a matter of fact, most of the time my feet never left the ground.

"...[if] the prophet had bid thee [do some] great thing,
wouldest thou not have done [it]?"
(2 Kings 5:13)

For a time when I was a little boy, I lived in Boulder, Colorado. We lived in a single-story ranch style home in what was then the country. We had horse property and a beautiful view of the Flat Irons, jetting up from the plains, declaring the beginning of the Rocky Mountains.

My parents owned an old red pick-up truck that we used to clean out the corral, haul the hay, and in the winter my dad would chain up the tires and pull us kids around the pasture on our eight-man toboggan. I learned to drive in that old truck, spreading manure around the field. On occasion, I even got to drive from our house up to the main road to pick up the mail. But I learned something even more important in that old red truck that I would like to share with you.

One afternoon our family loaded up the truck and went to visit some friends who lived nearby. At the conclusion of the visit we kids piled into the back of the pick-up for the ride home. (There were no laws against riding in the back in those days.) After two short blocks, Mom turned left and started down the steep hill toward home. Within seconds, the truck was swerving back and forth across the road. My sisters, my little brother and I were frightened as the truck went clear off the road into the borrow ditch and then fish tailed back across the road. The tires squealed when they hit the asphalt.

I looked through the back window and saw my mom wrestling the huge steering wheel on the old truck, pulling with both arms, trying to control it. (The old red truck didn't have power steering, and now, apparently no brakes either!) Mom looked over her shoulder, taking her eyes off the road for a split second. When our eyes met she yelled, "JUMP!"

The message was plain and simple, and she was serious.

"JUMP!" she shouted again.

There was no time for questions. She was my mother. She loved me and I knew it. I knew she cared for my well being. And at that age, I still thought she knew what was best for me. I jumped.

It wasn't until I had actually jumped, and sometime after the barrel roll over the tail-gate, but before I hit the asphalt that I actually considered the consequence of my decision.

After tumbling to a stop, I did a quick personal inventory. I was alive. I looked down the hill and saw our truck, speeding toward a dead end, on a crash course toward a busy road. I also noticed I was the only one who had jumped. Was my family going to be killed in a terrible crash? Would I be the only one who was saved, all because I did what I was told?

Children are so gullible. Is it their innocence or their complete faith and trust that allows them to be led and to follow directions? When my daughter Nichole was a toddler, I could get her to jump into my arms off the roof of our mobile home simply by saying, "Jump." Imagine that.

Last week I watched a movie with my girls. In the movie some young boys were playing a game of baseball in an empty lot. They had a real Major League coach. During the game, the coach noticed a little boy standing on top of an abandoned car, watching the game. Even though the boy had never played baseball and didn't know the rules, the coach put him in the game. When it was his turn to bat, the coach said, "Keep your elbows up, your eyes on the ball, and do everything I say." The coach lobbed the ball across the plate and yelled, "Swing!" The boy took his best shot. Crack! It was a hit! Not a home run but a hit just the same. The little boy made his way to first base and must have been thinking, *There's nothing to this game!* He realized that there was progress to be made by following the advice of the coach. The next batter approached the plate and took the pitch, crack! It was a big hit. The coach turned to the little boy who was standing on first base and yelled, "Run! Run home!" With a burst of excitement, the little boy ran to second base, but instead of turning toward third, he kept right on running, and running and running, right through the outfield and down the street. When the coach asked the other boys, "Where is he going?" They said, "Home. You told him to run home." All the way home the boy was repeating to himself, "Run home, run home, run home." He didn't know anything about the game, but he was eager to please the coach who cared enough to put him in the game.

Have you ever noticed that as we grow up, and supposedly get smarter, we tend to lose that childlike innocence; that willingness to trust and to follow. We want to be leaders, in charge of our own destiny. I remember seeing a billboard recently that said something to the effect that, "You have lived in your body all of your life; you should be in charge of it!" As we grow up, we start to question our parents, our teachers, our coaches. As members of the Church we have made covenants; to obey the commandments, sustain living prophets and to follow Christ. But many times we struggle with even the little things we are asked to do.

In 2 Kings, we read about Naaman the Syrian. *"Now Naaman, captain of the host of the king of Syria, was a great man with his master, and honorable,...he was also a mighty man in valor, [but he was] a leper."* By way of his wife's maid he learned about a prophet in Samaria, who could recover him of his leprosy. *"So Naaman came with his horses and his chariot, and stood at the door of the house of Elisha. And Elisha sent a messenger unto him, saying, Go and wash in Jordan seven times, and thy flesh shall come again to thee, and thou shalt be clean. But Naaman was wroth, and went away, and said, Behold, I thought, He will surely come out to me, and stand, and call on the name of the Lord his God, and strike his hand over the place, and recover the leper."* He proceeded to complain that the rivers in Damascus were better than all the rivers in Israel, and why couldn't he just wash in one of them. So he turned and went away in a rage. Lucky for him, his servant came and talked some sense into him. *"My father, if the prophet had bid thee do some great thing, wouldest thou not have done it? how much rather then, when he saith to thee, Wash, and be clean? Then he went down, and dipped himself seven times in Jordan, according to the saying of the man of God: and his flesh came again like unto the flesh of a little child, and he was clean." (2 Kings 5:1, 9-11, 13)*

"O that cunning plan of the evil one! O the vainness, and the frailties, and the foolishness of men! When they are learned they think they are wise, and they harken not unto the counsel of God (or his chosen leaders) for they set it aside, supposing they know of themselves, wherefore, their wisdom is foolishness and it profiteth them not. And they shall perish. But to be learned is good if they harken unto the counsels of God." (2 Nephi 9:28,29)

Much like the faith and trust of a little child, new members of the Church share that same determination to follow. With their new found testimony that God lives, that Jesus is the Christ, and that He loves us so much that He has called a living Prophet to guide us in these times of iniquity, they experience a burning feeling of love and appreciation. Who wouldn't want to follow? What a comfort that kind of testimony is to the soul. No wonder the Church of Jesus Christ of Latter-day Saints is the fastest growing church in the world. It is truly a marvelous work and a wonder.

Anja is a recent convert to the restored gospel of Jesus Christ. She entered the waters of baptism and took upon herself covenants to follow the Savior and her leaders. She made a commitment to stand as a witness of Christ at all times and in all places. She promised to mourn with those who mourn and succor those who stand in need of succor. She also made a commitment to serve her brothers and sisters when called upon to do so.

Anja was the new Laurels Class president in her ward. A few weeks ago it was her turn to conduct a Youth Committee Meeting. She must have felt a bit intimidated sitting at the head of the huge table in the High Council room. She was surrounded by most of the youth leaders in our stake and a group of her peers. In the Church we learn leadership skills by serving; not because we already know everything. Anja accepted the assignment and received some good counsel from her advisor on the finer points of how to successfully conduct a meeting.

The meeting went perfectly. When we were out of time, I leaned close to her and whispered, "We had better wrap this up." For the first time in the meeting, she appeared flustered. Her face turned red and hesitantly, she stood up and walked around the table behind the young man to her right. She said, "Jared, do you have anything else you would like to add?" Everyone was staring at her, wondering what in the world she was going to do. "No," Jared said. She then moved further around the table and stepped behind the next youth. "Do you have something you'd like to say?" she said. By this time everyone in the room was curious. "Anja, what are you doing?" someone asked. "I don't know," she said. Now she was even more embarrassed than before and said, "I was told that before closing the meeting I should go around the table and ask everyone if they had anything else they wanted to say." You can imagine the feeling in the room. At first a few people giggled, but most of us sat in silence. I'm sure my heart was not the only one in the room burning with the Spirit. Anja, who is originally from Bosnia, and moved here from Germany may not have understood all of the idioms used in the English language, or the given structure of every meeting and program of the Church, but she has a testimony we can all learn from. She is sincere in her commitment to do what she was asked to do, even when she doesn't quite understand why.

In Moses, we learn that after Adam and Eve were driven out of the Garden of Eden, Adam was obedient unto the commandments of the Lord. They were commanded to worship the Lord their God, and that they should offer the firstlings of their flocks as a sacrifice. *"And after many days an angel of the Lord appeared unto Adam, saying: Why dost thou offer sacrifices unto the Lord? And Adam said unto him: I know not, save the Lord commanded me." (Moses 5:6)*

I learned more than just how to drive in that old red truck back in Colorado. Sitting in the middle of that road, bruised and scraped, I learned that when you truly have faith in someone, you're willing to follow their counsel; whether they are your parents, your priesthood leaders, your Prophet, or your Savior. We may not always understand why, but maybe that's why, no matter how old we are, Heavenly Father refers to us as His children. We have a lot to learn. When He stands us up to the plate, in the game of life, He knows it's our first time on the field. All He asks of us is that we keep our elbows up, and do everything He says. If in the process we make a mistakes in front of our peers, remember, it is what's in our heart that counts.

To end my story about the old red truck, I must tell you that my mom was faced with two choices as she approached the bottom of the hill, left or right. Mom chose the right. She managed to make the turn at the bottom of the hill without rolling the truck. Old Red did a four-wheel-drift around the corner. How thankful I am that no cars were speeding down South Boulder Road at that exact moment. Turning uphill, she managed to avoid the danger of the traffic in the west-bound lane, and since a right turn headed her uphill again, she coasted safely to a stop. I love the lyrics to, *"Lord, I Would Follow Thee."*

Savior, may I learn to love thee, Walk the path that thou hast shown,
Pause to help and lift another, Finding strength beyond my own.
Savior, may I learn to love thee-Lord I would follow thee.
Who am I to judge another, when I walk imperfectly?
In the quiet heart is hidden, Sorrow that the eye can't see.
Who am I to judge another, Lord I would follow thee.
I would be my brothers keeper, I would learn the healers art,
To the wounded and the weary, I would show a gentle heart.
I would be my brothers keeper-Lord, I would follow thee.
Savior, may I love my brother, As I know thou lovest me,
Find in thee my strength my beacon, For thy servant I would be.
Savior, may I love my brother-Lord, I would follow thee.

Lyrics: Susan Evans McCloud, b. 1945. ©1985 LDS
Music: K. Newell Bayley, b.1939. ©1985 LDS

May we all have the faith to follow in obedience, and jump when the Spirit whispers in our ear.

Opportunityisnowhere

When I was a little boy my dad was a gymnastics coach.
I spent a lot of time in the gym watching and learning from the team.
Dad was a great teacher and he was a real stickler about one rule,
"Never say can't!"
Learning that lesson early was the best thing
that could have happened to me.

"...my grace is sufficient for all men that humble themselves before me;
for if they humble themselves before me, and have faith in me,
then will I make weak things become strong unto them."
(Ether 12:27)

In, *The Discourses of Marriner W. Merrill,* dated November 2, 1891, it states; "We have been under the necessity to conclude that there are a great many presiding men, many bishops in the Church, that are uninformed with regard to recommending their people to the temple. A very striking illustration was brought to my attention a few days ago in talking with a young man who came from a distance with his 'recommend' to the temple; and when he was questioned by the recording brother about when he was baptized, he did not know, he could not remember when he was baptized. Somebody failed to teach that young man properly. He came to me. I asked him, "Have you ever been baptized?" He said, "Well, I cannot remember. I do not know that I ever was baptized." "Well, you are here with a 'recommend' to obtain your blessings in the House of the Lord and you do not know whether you are a member of the church?" Now circumstances of this kind occur and we need not go far out of this stake to find something similar. I want to say to the presiding men of this Stake of Zion and to the presiding men of other stakes of Zion: "Do not send your young men to the temple unless you know that they are members of the church." Brother Joseph F. Smith inaugurated the policy some years ago which has never been annulled, and that was that all young people coming to the temple who had not attended to the ordinance of baptism before coming, should, prior to taking their endowments, first go and get baptized. It is inconvenient for young men coming perhaps one hundred miles to return home and get baptized, and we sometimes have to baptize them. Now, I say these things because they occupy my attention; and I see the importance of them as I engage with my brethren from day to day and from week to week." (Collected Discourses, Vol.2, Marriner W. Merrill, November 2, 1891)

Well, in a hundred and six years some things have changed and some things haven't. We don't have as many bishops sending people to the temple without first baptizing them, but it does require a recommend certifying our worthiness to enter the House of the Lord.

On the first Monday of every year I conduct individual interviews with all of my children. This year, after starting with a prayer I asked them questions like, "How's school?" and "How do you treat the other children at school?" I asked if they were having fun, or if they had any problems they wanted to talk about. I asked about our home life, "How are you getting along with your sisters? Are you happy?" Then I asked if

Mom and I were doing a good job teaching them about Jesus and Heavenly Father. I asked if they knew that Heavenly Father and Jesus loved them very much. I asked if they had testimonies and if they did the things they were asked to do at Church. I asked if they were paying a full tithing and if they were honest. At the end of the interview I told them that as their bishop, it was my opinion that they were each worthy of a temple recommend. I told them that if they would continue to live by the same high standards, that one day, they would be able to receive a recommend and be able to enjoy the blessing of temple attendance. I am thankful that my children attend Primary and sing songs like, *"Families Can Be Together Forever."*

> *"I have a family here on earth. They are so good to me. I want to share my life with them through all eternity. While I am in my early years, I'll prepare most carefully, So I can marry in God's temple for eternity. Families can be together forever through Heavenly Father's plan. I always want to be with my own family, and the Lord has shown me how I can. The Lord has shown me how I can."*
>
> Hymns: Families Can Be Together Forever. Words: Ruth Muir Gardner, b. 1927 © 1980 LDS. Music: Vanja Y. Watkins, b. 1938 © 1980 LDS

One day at work , I was interpreting in a classroom. My client was sitting in the back of the room, as far from the teacher as possible. I noticed a sign posted in the front of the classroom that read, "OPPORTUNITY IS NOWHERE." What a grim statement. It made me reflect on the countless number of Heavenly Father's children who harbor that same feeling of despair.

My daughter Sierra, was in a state of despair over her weekly spelling test at school. A passing grade in spelling was a goal she had seldom achieved. She hated spelling and had a genuine fear of those weekly tests while other students seemed to have no problem with them. It wasn't that she didn't study. She even took practice tests with Mom and Dad who made her write every missed word ten times. But she was convinced that she was different and unable to live up to her teacher's expectations.

Some members of the Church feel unsuccessful when it comes to living the principles of the gospel. They make mistakes, and some even fail personal tests on a weekly basis. I have met people who feel they are just different from the other members of the Church and therefore unable to live up to Heavenly Father's expectations.

It saddens me when I interview members of the Church who are convinced they are just not 'celestial material'. They think that because of prior mistakes or a period of inactivity they will never achieve the individual worthiness required to enter the Lord's House and receive His blessings.

How many of us are worthy in every way to enter the temple and participate in the temple ordinances? That is a question that requires some serious soul searching.

Yes, the standards are high. Yes, the requirements are strict. But if no unclean thing can enter the Kingdom of God, why would we expect less of a standard to enter the House of the Lord? Suppose the temple recommend interview was really a personal interview with the Savior. 'Are you worthy in every way to enter the Celestial Kingdom and participate in the ordinances thereof?'

Were it not for the miracle of forgiveness and the atoning sacrifice of the Savior, I would have to answer no to both questions. Repentance is a daily requirement for me. I, in and of myself, will never be worthy in every way. Only because of a loving, compassionate, and forgiving Father in Heaven is it possible for me to see the inside of his Holy House. And it is that same grace that provides me an opportunity to live with Him once more.

When it came to my daughter's spelling, the teacher didn't ever give up on her just because she failed a few tests. Nor did she look at her as a lost cause. Instead, she recognized Sierra for her efforts and her desire to succeed. The teacher tried a new approach. She gave Sierra a lap size chalkboard. She taught her the importance of copying the word from a correct source and then to trace the correct pattern with her finger, letter by letter, over and over until she began to understand, until she started to remember. Now Sierra looks forward to Fridays. She is considering competing in the Spelling Bee next year. She even meets me at the door on Friday evenings to tell me of her success. Sure, she still misses a word now and then but her teacher is proud of her progress and the fact that she never gives up.

At work I found myself interpreting back in that same classroom. This time my client was sitting closer to the front, closer to the teacher. That sign posted on the wall was easier to read and I noticed all the letters ran together. It could be read, "OPPORTUNITY IS NOWHERE," or "OPPORTUNITY IS NOW HERE." It really depends on how you look at it, or maybe on how close you are to the teacher. The opportunity is now here to prepare for a temple recommend. The opportunity is now here to participate in the saving ordinances in the Holy Temple.

Henry Ford said, "Whether you think you can or you can't... you're right!"

I say, "If you know you can...you will!"

Fly Away

Some people look at living the Commandments
as chains that hold them down.
I think the closer we live to them
the higher we can fly.

"...and the spirit lifted me up between the earth and the heaven,
and brought me in the visions of God..."
(Ezekiel 8:3)

"Hey Steve!...You can fly!" My brother sounded so excited I thought he was going to climb through the telephone line. He is always excited about something, but I could tell by his voice, this was going to be good.

He told me he had just read an article that said; "New tower in Las Vegas, designed to give you the thrill of a lifetime. People now have a chance to experience the freedom of flight, a chance to fly like a bird, without the use of wings; and more importantly, without the use of a parachute."

Naturally, I had to try it for myself. It was called Fly Away. From the outside it looked like a grain silo, tall and round. The inside walls were padded, and at different heights around the tower, there were tall skinny windows where people who weren't sure if they wanted to fly, could watch the action from a distance.

The floor of the tower was like a chain link fence. It was the only thing that protected the participants from a powerful, adjustable pitch, variable speed electric fan that was under the floor. It looked like the propeller of an airplane that was standing on its tail, ready to fly up through the tower. There was a padded bench against the wall that went all the way around the room. The ceiling looked just like the floor, a chain link fence. I guess it was supposed to prevent participants from being blown right out the vent and onto the street. There was one other window just to the right of the door that allowed the people in the tower to have eye contact with the man who operated the fan. He controlled the wind.

The very first thing they told me was that I was about to experience the most exciting thing I had ever done. The second thing they told me was to sign a release form in case I got killed having all that fun. On the wall were dozens of pictures, autographed by celebrities who had flown in the tower. They were smiling and appeared to have had a great time.

The cost to fly was two dollars per minute. Each person was required to attend ground school in order to learn how to fly. In the ground school, we watched a short video that explained some of the basics. Then we had a chance to practice what we had learned by lying face down, spread eagle on a bench. They gave us specific instructions on how to stay in control, and taught us how to maintain what they called a "stable position." It all seemed so easy there on the bench. No problem, a piece of cake. They told us that we were all capable of flying, if, we would follow their instructions. Anyone who failed to pay attention to the instructor would pay the price in the tower.

The next step was to get some protection. We were fitted with helmets, goggles, elbow pads, kneepads, the works. We wore big baggy jump suits, the kind real skydivers use when they jump out of planes. The suits were designed to be baggy so they could catch the wind and give lift. The two factors that affected how high you could fly were the size of your suit, (compared to your body-weight), and the speed of the wind.

I'll never forget the first time I entered the tower. Everything was so quiet. The instructor told us to stand on the padded bench around the outside of the tower and to spread out facing the center. He stood in the center of the room on the chainlink floor and stayed with us throughout the experience.

He decided it would be beneficial for us to watch him fly first, to give us an example of how it was supposed to be done. He was the only one of us who knew from experience the right way to fly.

I was surprised he didn't feel the need of all the protective gear that we had on. He was wearing tennis shoes, shorts and a tee shirt. He signaled the controller and the powerful fan motor cranked up. As the tower filled with the deafening roar of the motor, the instructor started jumping on the fence-like floor like a gymnast on a trampoline. He bounced up and down, going higher with every bounce. He started doing front flips and back flips and then all of the sudden, with one huge bounce he threw a one and three quarter back flip and didn't come down. He was flying.

The instructor made it look like so much fun. Instead of wearing a baggy flight suite to help keep him up in the air, the controller had turned the wind up so high, it wasn't much different than falling a hundred and twenty miles an hour out of the sky. He was floating above us like a helium balloon in the tower. His graceful flight quickly turned into a demonstration of spins and flips that astonished us. From one side of the tower to the other he darted around like a humming bird in complete control. He flew about half way up the tower and stood perpendicular to the wall looking down at us like a vertical wing-walker. Then he dove down on us like a hunting falcon and flew all the way back up to the fence-like ceiling where he hung from the ceiling like Spiderman. Then he dove at us again. When the demonstration was over the instructor signaled the controller and the fan slowed down. It was time for him to kick his little birdies out of the nest.

While standing on the floor, the teacher was not affected by the wind. It rushed right by him and out the ceiling vents. He stood in the center of the tower with his arms reaching toward us, coaxing us one at a time to join him in the wind.

There are a few important things to understand. In the tower, there is no wind on the walls. If you fly up against the wall, you can't stay there. You have to push back out into the wind. If you don't, you will come crashing back down (which explained the heavy padding on the bench). The most important thing to learn is really only common sense. You can't fly unless you enter the wind.

Everyone in the tower was taught the right way to enter the wind, but most of us didn't do very well at first. I was supposed to dive in, but logic told me it was more like diving off my living room couch onto the floor. My brain struggled with the concept and tried to convince me that if I dove off the bench, I'd do a belly-flop on the floor. Most people wanted to fly, but were afraid to make a commitment. They wanted to enjoy the flight but didn't have enough faith in the process. The result was failure. They may have made a brief contact with the teacher before they crashed into the wall and hit the bench.

The ones who made a sincere effort, and dove into the wind with their arms outstretched were on the right track. Every one of them found security in the grasp of the teacher. He helped them get their balance and find a stable flying position. When a student felt he was ready, he would let go for a second or two, just to see what it was like to be on his own. If the student failed to maintain a stable position, the result was painful. They would veer off to one side or the other, and inevitably crash into the wall (and you know what that means, splat!) Sometimes before a student managed to fly too far away, the teacher was able to reach out and grab them by an arm or leg and help them get stable again. But if they got too far out of reach, they suffered the consequences. The part I liked most was when the teacher would spin someone high above his head and put his finger on their stomach. It was like they were the basketball and he was a Harlem Globetrotter.

The instructor went around the room inviting each of us to join him in the wind. At last it was my turn. The first step was not as easy to take as I had anticipated. I half-heartedly leaned forward and stepped off the bench. I fell face first at the teacher's feet. He helped me up and gave me another chance. From the bench, I looked into his beckoning eyes, his arms were reaching for me, his hands motioning me to enter the wind. I knew from my ground schooling that I had to have enough faith to trust the wind. I had already proved how not to do it, just like I had done so often in other aspects of my life.

Suddenly, I dove straight for the teacher. Once we locked hands I was no longer afraid of the wall. It was really quite a wonderful feeling to be lifted by the wind, surrounded by such incredible power. But as with all the other students, the instructor knew I would not learn the real wonder of flight without experiencing a little time on my own.

When you were a kid, did you ever stick your hand out of the car window when you were going down the highway? (Do not try this.) You know what I mean. You shape your hand like the wing of a plane, then by altering the pitch just the slightest bit, it almost rips your arm off! That's the basic description of a modified "stable flight position." One second you're enjoying the freedom of flight, and the next, your looking up from the bench, hurt and embarrassed.

After crashing a few times I learned the basics of how to maintain a stable flying position. Little by little I improved until I was flying around the tower doing flips and spins under the watchful eyes of those who were observing from the outside of the tower.

"And he put forth the form of an hand, and took me by a lock of mine head; and the spirit lifted me up between the earth and the heaven, and brought me in the visions of God..." (Ezekiel 8:3)

Nurtured in the gospel of Jesus Christ, we are taught all that is necessary to be lifted by the Holy Spirit. Ours is the opportunity to enjoy the freedom of flight found in the Plan of Salvation. The Commandments define our protection, and only when we turn from them, do we get hurt. The power can be all around us, but if we lack the faith and are unwilling to enter the wind, we will never rise above the earth and accomplish all we have potential to do. The Savior stands forever waiting, with His arms outstretched, beckoning, *"Come unto me, all [ye] that labour and are heavy laden, and I will give you rest." (Matthew 11:28)* We may stumble and we may fall, but He will always give us another chance. He allows us the agency to fly on our own in order to learn for ourselves, but His Spirit is never far away when we need help getting back into a stable flying position. Dive in, *"Humble yourselves in the sight of the Lord, and he shall lift you up." (James 4:10)*

A Real Masterpiece

Every now and then you meet a real Saint.
Thanks wasn't enough, so I wrote this for Thelma.

"And the Lord sent an angel..."
(2 Chronicles 32:21)

In August of 1991, I was called to serve as bishop of the Carmichael Ward. It was the second time my wife Janice and I had an opportunity to serve the Lord together. I would attend my meetings, visit the sick and the widows, and Janice would carry a heavier load around the house. She had vivid memories of Sunday mornings when we lived in Colorado, getting our daughters ready for church by herself. She would drive the children forty-eight miles to Leadville Colorado, over Climax Pass to attend the branch where I was serving as branch president. Since I had meetings early in the morning, we took two cars. When I left everyone was asleep so I didn't get to help out much around the house on Sundays. I usually stayed in Leadville after the meetings to do interviews, so that I didn't have to commute as often during the week.

Janice has always sustained me in all my callings and this time in Carmichael wasn't going to be an exception. We had five daughters under the age of eight and the thought of getting them ready for church, and keeping them reverent during Sacrament Meeting by herself must have been on her mind when she told the stake president she would sustain me.

Heavenly Father always helps us fulfill our callings when we are willing to serve. And He regularly uses His willing servants to accomplish these marvelous tasks.

Shortly after I was given the responsibility of the ward, I called a new Relief Society president, Naomi Harper. She was sensitive to the promptings of the Holy Ghost which allowed Heavenly Father to use her as a tool in assisting my wife with the added responsibility of being the bishop's wife. There was a sister in our ward named Thelma Black who usually sat in the back of the chapel. She was a widow and her children were grown. Sister Harper approached her and asked if she would be willing to sit with the bishop's family and help Janice with the children during sacrament meeting. Sister Black willingly became another tool for Heavenly Father and the gospel was in action. Sister Black has been sitting with my girls for seven years and has been a wonderful blessing to our family.

People often comment on how reverent my children are in church. And though Janice and I have tried to teach them reverence, having Sister Black sit with them has made a big difference in their behavior. Sister Black brings quiet things for the babies to look at. She holds them, loves them, and makes the occasional trips to the rest room with them. She calls my girls on the phone during the week just to say hello, or to plan outings and parties. She takes my girls to the mall, the park, and the movies. She has come to stay with the children while Janice and I attend the temple or go out on date night. My girls call her on the phone, and go over to her house to play and to help her clean. They have sleep-overs too. She has planned and put on birthday parties, complete with decorating the house and providing personalized birthday cakes for every one of them. She has truly become an important part of our family. One time when she was watching the little girls, I came home and found her under the table playing with them. There was a blanket draped over the table which served as a fort or clubhouse of some kind.

I am thankful for an inspired Relief Society president and a sister in my ward who has been a sharp tool in the hands of the Master to accomplish a great work. Sister Black is a great example of how a ward family can pull together and accomplish anything. Sister Harper is a great example of how inspired leaders can affect the lives of the members they have stewardship over. Not only was it easier for me to do my calling when I knew my wife was not alone to manage the children, but my children have developed a relationship with Sister Black that they will never forget.

Sister Black has found the joy that comes when we loose ourselves in the service of others. *"And behold, I tell you these things that ye may learn wisdom; that ye may learn that when ye are in the service of your fellow beings ye are only in the service of your God." (Mosiah 2:17)*

I know Sister Black loves my children deeply. She told me a story once of why she loves little children so much. She said, "They always tell you straight, they don't fluff it up or say what they think you want to hear."

One morning in sacrament meeting Sister Black was sitting next to my daughter, Sierra, who noticed Sister Black wasn't singing the hymns. Sierra said, "Sing, Sister Black!" So, in an effort to set a good example for the girls, Sister Black sang. Shortly thereafter, Sierra turned her head, looked up at Sister Black with her big blue eyes and said, "Please don't sing Sister Black." In another Sacrament Meeting, a member of the bishopric was encouraging the ward members to join the choir. Sierra turned to Sister Black and innocently said, "Not you Sister Black!" Well you might guess how I would have reacted if I had heard that kind of a comment from one of my girls. But Sister Black loved it. She cherishes the honesty of the children. My little Sierra may not have realized how blunt she was that morning, but she loves Sister Black with a pure love. There are no reservations and no strings attached. And every one of my girls feel the same way.

Picture this. It was stake conference and I was sitting on the stand about to share my testimony at the request of Elder Joe J. Christensen, our visiting General Authority. I had just been sustained as the second counselor to our new stake president. I was overwhelmed by the call, and was looking out into a cultural hall that was packed with stake members. I felt small and inadequate. I kept saying to myself, *"I will go; I will do the things the Lord commands. I know the Lord provides a way; he wants me to obey."*

Nephi's Courage. Words and music: Bill N. Hansen, Jr., b. 1952, and Lisa T. Hansen, b. 1958 (© 1986 by Wilford N. Hansen, Jr., and Lisa Tensmeyer Hansen.)

That was when I looked up and saw Sister Black sitting in the second row with my family. Chandler, my two-year-old, was sitting on her lap. I was reminded once again how Heavenly Father provides for me. He has always been there for me when I try to be humble and show a little faith.

Chandler had just finished meticulously placing two or three full sheets of stickers all over Sister Black's face. Sister Black sat patiently holding Chandler so that Janice could join me on the stand with the other members of the new stake presidency and their wives. Chandler kept rearranging the stickers, *hmmm, I think this one would look better on her ear than her nose.* It was as though she were a student of Rembrandt's, creating a masterpiece. I know that Heavenly Father had already done the creating when it came to Sister Black. She is a true masterpiece. She is a kind and loving daughter of God. She gives selflessly and is a true example of a Latter-day Saint.

Pier Pressure

After I joined the Church, I continued to play music in night clubs for about five and a half months. Saturday nights we played until two o'clock in the morning. If the town we were playing in was close enough to Glenwood Springs, Colorado we packed up our equipment and drove home. I would fall into bed at about six A.M. and get up at nine to go to Church. I had long hair and my eyes were always red from the smokey bars. My ears would still be ringing from our band's music, as I sang the Hymns of Zion. The members of the Glenwood Ward welcomed me with open arms every week. Every time I prayed about my employment situation, the answer I received was to quit the band. Every time, I ignored the answer. I loved the band. I loved the guys in the band.

I will never forget sitting in a car by myself at about three-thirty in the morning. It was in Steamboat Springs, Colorado. It was freezing cold out and I was crying because I realized what I had to do. I quit the band. It was the hardest thing I've ever done.

It was a great first step to listening to the spirit of inspiration instead of listening to the ringing in my ears.

"...leap for joy: for, behold, your reward [is] great in heaven..."
(Luke 6:23)

There have been several times in my life when I fell victim to peer pressure. I'm not proud of the choices I made and have since learned that I would have been better off if I had listened to the still small voice of the Spirit, rather than the coaxing bellow of the multitude.

The day was like most Southern California summer days. There was a constant breeze blowing onto the beach, blue skies and a parade of waves that never seemed to quit. The waves weren't big, but judging from the crowded beaches, the number of swimmers, boogie boards, and surfers, this was the place to be.

It was the week my family moved into town. Southern California was an exciting place for a boy from Colorado. The first thing I did was go to the beach to enjoy some fun in the sun. I went with my sister Kathie and her boyfriend Neil, who helped us drive one of our cars on the migration west. Avoiding the crowded waves of LaJolla Shores, we walked north on the beach to Scripps. There we spent part of the time catching rays, and the other part, bodysurfing on the south side of the pier. While we were treading water just outside the break, waiting for some good waves, Neil noticed a stairway that climbed from the water to the top of the pier. He was disappointed that there was a locked gate to keep people out. He also noticed a chain-link ladder hanging from the pier. Neil came up with the bright idea to climb it. Right away I didn't have a good feeling about his plan. The feeling was even stronger when I climbed past the sign that said, "KEEP OFF." But I was following my older sister who was following her boyfriend and we ignored the warning. We climbed to the top.

The view from on top of the pier was incredible. All my apprehensions faded and I took advantage of my new perspective. I even forgot the uneasy feeling I had while climbing past the warning sign. We were on the top. There were lots of other people wandering around on the end of the pier. With the sun beating down on us and the breeze to cool us off, it was like being on top of the world.

We were sitting on the top of the railing that was designed to keep the fisherman from falling off the pier. From there we could see all the way to Children's Cove. We had a perfect view of the big ships headed north from San Diego Harbor and a bird's-eye view of the surfers, challenging the elements as they surfed dangerously close to the pier.

Without warning, Neil stood up on the railing and jumped. It looked like he was falling in slow motion and seemed to take forever before he hit the Pacific below. When he finally disappeared into the water I got a sick feeling like he had killed himself. I stared at the foamy spot below for long time before he finally popped up laughing. "Come on, it's great!" he shouted. He was the craziest person I knew. In my heart and mind I knew that no amount of money, and no five guys could force me off that pier. I turned to tell Kathie that I wouldn't jump if my life depended on it, but before I could open my mouth she stood up and jumped.

I was stunned. Never in a million years would I have considered the possibility that she would jump. I would have bet money against it. And before I could rationalize her actions, she was waving her arms and laughing, "Come on...chicken?"

I had a sick feeling in my stomach. I started to question my resolve not to jump. Was I a wimp? Was it really that high? They were still alive. They hadn't died. I think I could have told Neil, "NO!" But after my sister jumped, my masculinity was at stake.

There was no mistaking the voice of warning that rang loud and clear in my head, but my ego had been crushed and I was reluctantly, but assuredly going to cast aside my better judgment.

Standing on that railing on the end of Scripps Pier in the summer of 1967, I made a bad choice. I jumped. That started a bad habit that made the next thirteen years of my life a very rough road. It was the day I learned to succumb to peer pressure.

During the summer months of my high school years, my boss and I used to spend all of our spare time in the Colorado River. His dad worked at the Shoshone Dam and that meant we could access a section of the river that no one else could. It was a water skier's paradise.

One afternoon I was skiing with my brother Keith and his friend Charley. They noticed a cliff over a railroad tunnel on the far side of the river. It was their bright idea to do some cliff jumping off the rocks. After we checked how deep the river was using a ski rope and a rock, we swam over to the cliff and climbed up. There were several different places to jump from varying heights, but Keith and his friend kept right on climbing. I made a few suggestions like, "Okay, this looks good right about here," but they continued to climb, until they reached the top. I followed.

When I walked over to the edge and looked down at the boat, it didn't take a second for me to decide, "I wouldn't jump off here without a parachute!" With one step and a leap, Charley hurled himself over the edge of the cliff. He didn't jump, he did a gainer (a backwards flip facing forward). I almost died. I was in total shock. He was a punk kid, how did he do that? Then the sick feeling came, I'm not going to jump, I'm not going to jump, I'm not going to jump. And without saying a word, which seems to be the style of these whack-o-jumpers, my little brother launched himself into a beautiful swan dive off the cliff.

Remember, this was not the first time I had been left on the edge of reality by my family and friends. Looking down at my brother in the river was like a dream. I heard him shouting, "Come on, it's fun. It will be all right. Don't worry." But I wasn't sure I was all there. My mind was reeling. This time I was educated. I was smarter. I yelled down my decision on the matter, "You're nuts. I'm not jumping! No way!"

I turned from the cliff and headed back to safety. I headed back the way I came. I felt good about my decision and rather proud of myself for being secure about it. I didn't care what they thought. Just because my baby brother jumped, didn't mean I had to. I made my own decision and I was willing to live with it. Besides, it felt good to say no. What I wasn't prepared for was how difficult my actual retreat was going to be.

I started to climb down but any experienced climber can tell you, going down is twice as hard as climbing up. I suddenly realized that climbing down was going to put me at greater risk than I expected. I stood the chance of falling to my death on the rocks below, or onto the railroad tracks, neither of which sounded very good. I took a stroll around the top of the cliff looking for another way down but there wasn't one. I had two choices. Risk life and limb by climbing down the way I came up, or follow my brother and his buddy 'Geronimo' to my death. I didn't like either choice but after a frustrating mental battle, I decided that the water looked softer than the rocks. I was distraught over the fact that even though this time, I was victorious over the peer pressure, I was going to end up jumping anyway because I had come too far to go back.

I was going to jump, but it took me forever. I stood there staring over the edge, waiting for my courage to come, but it never did. When I took that grievous step there was no courage involved. I jumped only to complete the inevitable.

In high school I had a friend who was confined to a wheelchair because he dove out of a boat and broke his back. He only dove about five feet. It wasn't the height from which he dove that put him in a wheelchair, it was the rock lurking below the surface of the water. I had to try something to protect myself. I was so nervous about hitting the bottom,

I tried to do a 'J-type' entry and in order to avoid going too deep. Over anticipating the landing, I hit the water in what is best described as a half seat-drop. When I managed to get back in the boat, I watched my legs turn black and blue from my knees to my waist, while Keith and Charley made a few more jumps.

There will always be someone willing to take you over the cliffs in life. There will always be one willing to go first to show you that it's easy. They will tell you it's fun, and laughing and coaxing, they will lure you into falling into a consuming ocean of sin and sorrow. Be careful how far you are willing to let someone else lead you past the warning signs. When your heart tells you, this looks like a good spot right here, make the right choice.

There is strength in making your decisions well in advance, long before you are standing on the top rail in a dangerous position. If you commit early to follow the commandments, and to uphold the standards that Christ would have you follow, it doesn't matter what anyone else says or thinks.

"Rejoice ye in that day, and leap for joy: for, behold,
your reward [is] great in heaven..."
(Luke 6:23)

The Little Ones

When I joined the Church and started living the Word of Wisdom, I needed something to occupy my attention. I needed to replace some bad habits with a good one. I chose Sign language. For the last seventeen years I've been learning to sign and loving it. I've been interpreting for the last seven years and full time for the last three. Even though I'm starting to get the hang of it, once in a while I see signs I don't understand.

For the last fifteen years I have been a father. It is the best of my blessings. Every birth brought tears, and every year has brought joy. Even though I think I'm getting the hang of it, I still see signs I don't understand.

"And it came to pass that he did teach and minister unto the children of the multitude of whom hath been spoken, and he did loose their tongues, and they did speak unto their fathers great and marvelous things, even greater than he had revealed unto the people..."
(3 Nephi 26:14)

Not long after Janice and I were married, we visited the home of her uncle, John Mattson. There we received the warmest of welcomes. They were excited to see little 'Jan' all grown up, and with a husband and everything. After Aunt Bev fed us a big meal, we settled into the family room to relax and get to know each other better.

The Mattsons have a large family and to this day I'm not sure if I can get all their names straight, but there was one part of our visit I will never forget. It was obvious that these children were their parents' pride and joy. It made me anticipate the day when I would enjoy such a blessing.

One by one John and Bev introduced me to their children. They told us every detail about what their children were involved in and recited all their major accomplishments. It reminded me of when I was growing up. If there was company in the Burrows home, that was when I had to walk around the house on my hands, or do back handsprings in the middle of the living room floor. When my wife was a little girl, at times like that her twin brother Jon, would amaze visitors by standing on his face. *He doesn't have a bone in his nose, and he did a unique version of a headstand.*

The living room floor of the Mattson's home became a stage for each of the children to perform. Uncle John is one of those BYU season-ticket-holding, 'Sports Dads.' After a demonstration of strength and agility from the older boys, John tried to get me to wrestle with, 'Salt Lake's finest.' I didn't want to embarrass myself in front of my new bride, so I declined (even though he was in grade school).

When it came to their little four year old, Jacob's turn, Aunt Bev asked him if he wanted to read his dinosaur book for me. His eyes lit up and he disappeared from the room. I knew I was in for a treat, not because I love dinosaurs or anything, but because of the look of enthusiasm worn by their whole family. Jacob bolted back into the room and climbed upon my lap. "All About Dinosaurs," he said. He opened the book to the first page and there at the top was a picture of a dinosaur. He started telling me about the Stegosaurus and how it had two rows of alternating, upright bony plates that developed along its back. I was amazed how perceptive he was, and how much detail he was gleaning from the picture. He continued with his description of the massive creature, and told me several other details about its activities and eating habits. Jacob turned the page and started telling me about the Brontosaurus; again, in great detail. I was genuinely impressed. He knew more about dinosaurs than anyone I knew. I looked up from the picture at his parents and siblings, and they were beaming with admiration. "This is one smart little kid," I said. But there was something in their expressions that made me think I was missing something. I looked back to the book and Jacob was on to Theropods. This time I looked down at the words and was shocked to realize that the little boy was reading. He was articulate in his pronunciations of the difficult words and phrases. I remained skeptical of his ability to read until, time after time he turned the page and never missed a word. I read along with him, "The Tyrannosaurus is the largest of the Theropods, which grew to a weight from five to six metric tons (about ten thousand pounds,) a height of six meters (eighteen feet,) and a length of fifteen meters (forty-five feet.)" I didn't believe it. I was in shock.

After the family had a good laugh, they confessed that I was the brunt of a practical joke. Jacob's real talent wasn't reading at a college level, it was his incredible memory. He loved dinosaurs and his parents bought him the book that came with an audio tape. It was a great gift for a child who wasn't reading yet but who could enjoy listening to the tape while looking at the pictures. There was a distinctive chime that let the child know when it was time to turn the pages. Little Jacob loved his book so much that he spent all of his spare time gazing at the pictures of the massive creatures, and turning the pages at each tone.

At first the narration was only back-ground noise to the little boy, whose real fascination was in the size and strength of the creatures. He couldn't get over how long their necks were, or how sharp their horns were. He especially liked their big teeth. Little by little he picked up on specific words from the tape, and started associating them with the pictures on the page. Those select words became phrases and well, the rest is obvious. Jacob, by turning the pages and looking at the pictures, could quote the entire book. I learned that day of the ability, the capacity, and the desire that children have for learning.

About a week after I was baptized, I got a ride into town from a member of my ward. I don't remember the brother's name or even why I needed the ride, but I will always remember his daughter, Tearza. The little girl sat between us in the truck and her dad said to her, "This is Brother Burrows, he was just baptized last week. Why don't you teach him about the Articles of Faith." This little girl who couldn't have been five, handed me a card that listed the thirteen Articles of Faith. She didn't hesitate in responding to her fathers request. "Number one; We believe in God the Eternal Father, and in His son Jesus Christ, and in the Holy Ghost." She went on, "Number two; We believe that men will be punished for their own sins, and not for Adam's transgressions." All thirteen Articles of Faith, one after another poured flawlessly from this curly headed child. Occasionally, I looked up from the card I was holding in disbelief, only to see her baby blue eyes and her smile. I still see that image when ever I read the Articles of Faith.

These examples of children learning incredible things at such a young age are not unique. Most parents can tell similar stories about their own children. Children are born to learn and are like sponges that absorb everything around them. Parents are shocked everyday by the things their children remember. They recognize streets and signs, buildings and other landmarks they might not have passed for several years. They remember the words to songs, and commercial jingles. They pick up things Mom said or Dad said, or even the kids at school. They love to learn. They always learn. They will learn. And what they learn depends a great deal upon the environment in which they are raised.

The prophets for ages have taught us to look to the Savior's example, in all that we say and do. As we consider our responsibility to teach our children, and to follow the Savior's example in doing so, we may have a picture in our minds that represents how the Savior was when He was with the children. There are some paintings that depict the Savior with children. Many copies are hanging in meetinghouses around the world. My personal favorite, 'Behold Your Little Ones' was painted by Crystal Haueter, of Fair Oaks, California. Her painting tells the story of the Savior blessing the children on the American Continent. I can't help thinking about it every time I read; *"And it came to pass that [the Savior] commanded that their little children should be brought. So they brought their little children and set them down upon the ground round about him, and Jesus stood in the midst; and the multitude gave way till they had all been brought unto him. And it came to pass that when they had all been brought, and Jesus stood in the midst, he commanded the multitude that they should kneel down upon the ground. And it came to pass that when they had knelt upon the ground, Jesus groaned within himself, and said: Father, I am troubled because of the wickedness of the people of the house of Israel. And when he had said these words, he himself also knelt upon the earth; and behold he prayed unto the Father, and the things which he prayed cannot be written, and the multitude did bear record who heard him. And after this manner do they bear record: The eye hath never seen, neither hath the ear heard, before, so great and marvelous things as we saw and heard Jesus speak unto the Father; And no tongue can speak, neither can there be written by any man, neither can the hearts of men conceive so great and marvelous things as we both saw and heard Jesus speak; and no one can conceive of the joy which filled our souls at the time we heard him pray for us unto the Father. And it came to pass that when Jesus had made an end of praying unto the Father, he arose; but so great was the joy of the multitude that they were overcome. And it came to pass that Jesus spake unto them, and bade them arise. And they arose from the earth, and he said unto them: Blessed are ye because of your faith. And now behold, my joy is full. And when he had said these words, he wept, and the multitude bare record of it, and he took their little children, one by one, and blessed them, and prayed unto the Father for them. And when he had done this he wept again; And he spake unto the multitude, and said unto them: Behold your little ones. (3 Nephi 17:11-23)*

The Savior's plan was to set an example for us by the way he lived. His plan was to atone for our sins and give His life for us. He wanted us to have the ability to choose for ourselves whether or not we believe. I literally believe that it is our choice. No one can make that choice for another person.

As a father, no matter what I try to teach my children, they will learn more from me by the way I live and the things I do than what I tell them. They will learn from their own experiences, and from the environment around them.

It doesn't make sense to me when parents think they need to place all the choices of the world before their children in order to respect their free agency. I prefer whenever possible to place good choices before my children. The idea that we can shield our children from every bad choice is unreasonable, and 'the world' will work overtime to present those choices anyway. I've heard parents say, "If I don't let my children watch a few 'R' rated movies now, when they grow up and move out, they will want to watch 'X' rated movies." I have heard people say, "If I insist that my child attends Church, Mutual, or even Seminary, it will just push them away from me. I want them to love me, so I let them do what they want."

If you tell your children not to watch 'R' rated movies, but you do, what will they learn? If you tell them the temple is important, and you don't go, what will they think? If you tell them to dress conservatively, and you don't, what will they do? Tithing, honesty, and morality are all lessons we teach our children everyday, whether we know it or not. This familiar primary song is sung by parents every day around the world, loud and clear, even if they can't carry a tune.

> *Do as I'm doing, follow follow me.*
> *Do as I'm doing , follow follow me.*
> *If I do it high or low,*
> *If I do it fast or slow.*
> *Do as I doing follow follow me,*
> *Do as I'm doing follow follow me.*

Children's Song Book, Page 276, Words: Anon. Music: Folk style.
(© 1963 by D.C. Heath and Company.)

The phrase, 'Actions speak louder than words,' doesn't mean that if we attend church on Sunday and do our callings, that it will make up for the comments we make at the dinner table about Brother and Sister So-n-So, or the time we bad-mouthed the bishop on the way home from church.

Our children are looking at the pages of life with fascination, and day after day they are picking up the words and phrases that they hear. Don't be surprised if at a very young age they are able to quote page after page of your book. They may not leave out a thing.

To be safe we: *"...should be anxiously engaged in a good cause..."*
(D&C 58:7)

"And all thy children shall be taught of the Lord;
and great shall be the peace of thy children."
(3 Nephi 22:13)

What's Flapping Behind You?

You'll notice I write a lot of stories about my brother, Keith.
I could fill more than one book with my love for him.
I want to learn how to expand that brotherly love to my neighbors.
This story is about Keith, but when I read it,
it is my life hanging on the wing of that plane.

"And I saw the dead, small and great, stand before God; and the books were opened: and another book was opened, which is the book of life: and the dead were judged out of those things which were written in the books, according to their works."
(Revelation 20:12)

One night I was sitting at my computer, looking for an inspirational story hiding between the rows of letters on my keyboard. My phone rang and it was my brother, Keith. He wanted me to know what it feels like to face the possibility of death and how important it is to prepare for such and occasion. His story goes like this:

It didn't seem to matter that my hands were sweaty. My grip had never felt so strong. The sound of the plane's engine was oddly distant as I concentrated on the events that would occupy the next few moments of my life. I had just stepped onto the landing gear of a Cessna 172, and hand-over-hand, worked my way out under the wing. It was my first sky diving experience. For the first time in my life I had come face-to-face with fear!

I didn't find myself in that position by accident. Many times since I was a boy, I had discussed the idea of sky-diving. I had visualized the moment, even dreamt about it. I guess what they say is true. All actions begin as a thought.

Throughout my life, I have been quick to seek a thrill; climbing and skiing fourteen thousand foot peaks, cliff jumping, parasailing, hanggliding, rock climbing, even speed skiing over a hundred miles an hour. But now, perched on the wing of a plane, with five thousand feet of nothing between me and Mother Earth, this was the crème de la crème, the big kahuna, the sit-up-and-take-notice, real no kiddin', yaba-daba-doooooooo. *Put it this way, it was serious.*

I started to ask myself, "Why am I here? What is going to happen to me? Had the ground school been adequate? Did I pay sufficient attention? Did they teach me all that I needed to know? Will I make the right decisions in the time allotted me?"

The ground school had been brief, yet effective. They had successfully planted a seed of fear in me, and out on the wing that seed had grown into a mighty oak. The instructor had spent the majority of the time drilling us on the variety of malfunctions that could occur while sky diving. He said, "Now if your chute doesn't open...do this...and do that..." *Suddenly, I felt an urgent need to dash home and see if I had left the iron plugged in.* I had a completely different picture in my mind of what ground school would be like. Something more 'low key'. I expected to learn what kind of shoes to wear, and how to steer my chute, thus increasing the odds of landing in the same state I jumped over. I was not prepared for the blatant admission of the danger involved. I figured they would sweep all that under the rug and keep everything upbeat and positive. Instead, the jump master said, "Based on statistics, and the number of students in our class, one of you will experience a malfunction." No sooner had the words rolled off his tongue than I was thinking, *Great...It will be me. Just then it occurred to me that Channel 40 was showing that rerun of the final episode of "Little House On the Prairie," I thought, I can't miss it! I gotta go!...see ya!* But the fact was, I was in too deep to get out. I was past the get-off-speed and would have to ride this one out.

The jump-master taught us the difference between high speed malfunctions and low speed malfunctions, and even as a newcomer to the sport with limited knowledge, I was ready to vote for a low speed malfunction. We learned that it is only a matter of seconds between the time you let go of the plane and when you reach the hard deck (two thousand feet above the ground,) at which point you better have your chute open. The sequence of events and decisions that have to be made before that point, must be quick and precise. Once again, I voted for a slow speed malfunction.

I listened carefully to the instructions that were given to the young lady who jumped before me. From the ground one of the instructors was assigned to watch our progress, and he was giving the girl who jumped instructions. All of us could hear his promptings through the headphones in our helmets. The idea was that he would talk us through the decisions we would have to make. He would help us to have an enjoyable experience. "Turn left," he told her. "Now right...try your brakes...okay, now enjoy yourself." It should have been me out there. I really wanted to be the first one out of the plane. I never could sit still for five minutes, but mostly it was my way of dealing with the fear. And just for the record, I couldn't watch when the young lady left the plane. To make things worse, after she jumped, the plane entered some clouds and they had to spend the next thirty minutes looking for a hole in the clouds for me to jump through.

"Climb out to the tape and just let go," the instructor said. Now, perched under the wing, I was staring at the ragged piece of duct tape which marked the spot. I told myself that hundreds, maybe thousands of others had clung to this very spot, stared at this very tape and lived to tell about it. Surely I would tell my grandchildren about this. Or would I? Just before I was about to jump, the reception in my headphones went from bad to worse. Then it quit. This was no time for Murphy's Law to manifest itself, and for some reason letting go was no longer my first choice. With a desperate gaze, I looked at the jump master who was still in the plane. I realized that getting back into the plane would be more dangerous than jumping. Could I jump without the promptings from the instructor on the ground? And after all, it had been my decision to turn down a tandem jump (basically as a passenger), or an accelerated free-fall (accompanied by two jump-masters). It was my bright idea to do this thing on my own.

I knew I had listened closely in my ground school class. I wondered if they taught me everything I needed to know. Mentally, I went through the steps. Let go, arch, stare at the tape and count to five, look back, assess the situation, unstow the handles, left turn, right turn, hit the brakes, enjoy the ride. At fifteen hundred feet turn down wind, at a thousand feet turn left, at five hundred feet turn left again, land into the wind, pulling the brakes to stall out into a smooth landing. Again I rehearsed. Let go, count, look, reach, pull, but still the haunting phrase rang in my ears, "One of you will have a malfunction." I started over; let go, arch, count, look back. What if the pilot chute doesn't open? Look, reach, and pull the main chute. When it opens, I would have five to ten seconds to look back and decide if I was willing to land whatever was flapping behind me.

I rehearsed in my mind some of the possible problems I might face at that point. My lines could get twisted, the slider could get hung up or I could have problems with the end sails. I wondered, What if the whole chute looks like a streamer? Without hesitating, I would have to cut it loose, look to make sure I was clear of the discarded chute, and reach for and pull my reserve chute. Now, the next thing the instructor taught me, I never really understood. He said, "At that point, look back to assess the situation." Like it was really going to make a difference. I only had one reserve chute, and if that baby was a streamer, my options were limited. The jump master suggested, "If that happens to you, aim for the nicest car in the parking lot." When I asked him why. His reply was, "Then you won't hit my old pick-up truck!"

Trizel, Trazel, Truzel, Trome, Time for this one to come home. I was waiting for someone to wake me up from this bad dream.

I let go. I arched and counted in my head, one, two, three, four, five. I looked back. The pilot chute had worked and the main chute was open. Then I saw it. My lines were twisted! Fortunately it was a low-speed malfunction. I reached up and while kicking and jerking my legs, I managed to pull the lines apart. I spun around about three times like we used to do on the swing sets at school. *It was more fun back then.* I unstowed my handles to perform a controllability check and suddenly I noticed my altimeter was facing the ground. That was no good. I let go of my handles and turned it over...FIVE HUNDRED FEET!...ALREADY! So much for the systematic approach on the landing. I was going to get reacquainted with Mother Earth, and fast.

Well, I guess it's obvious I lived through the landing, but it wasn't pretty. Have you ever seen the movie *Rescuers Down Under?* My landing was a lot like the goofy bird who crash landed on the roof in the movie. It was Albatross Airlines all over again.

Much like it was for Keith hanging on that wing, at different times we find ourselves doing some serious soul searching. We ask ourselves, Am I ready to meet my Savior? Have I repented for all of my transgressions? Have I done any good in the world today? What have I done with the talents that Heavenly Father entrusted me with? Have I kept the covenants that I made when I entered the waters of baptism?" In a life and death situation, most of us would pour our heart out in prayer, asking for guidance in all of our remaining decisions.

I'm glad my brother lived through his sky-diving adventure. I'm glad he called me first to share his feelings about it. His experience has helped me to understand and bring more clearly into focus, just how precious each day is. From now on when I look over my shoulder at my past, I will be considering my ability to land all that is flapping behind me. I will ask myself, Have I paid sufficient attention to the things I have been taught? Will I be able to control my flight, making all the right turns? Will I hear the whisperings of the Holy Ghost, that will prompt me and guide me to the place I want to go? Will I have an enjoyable experience? Or will my reception be poor? Will my lines get twisted? Or will I be at the mercy of the wind and experience a reckless crash?'

In the Old Testament there is a lesson to be learned when Isaiah the son of Amoz went to see Hezekiah. Hezekiah was very sick and Isaiah told him, *"...Set thine house in order: for thou shalt die, and not live." (Isaiah 38:1)*

We may not be *'...sick unto death.'* as Hezekiah was, but we will all have an interview with the Savior. When I have visualized what that experience will really be like, I have truly felt His love. Not because I am without sin, but because I have felt His sweet and comforting Spirit testify to me of His desire to forgive me. He hears my prayers and will forgive me when I forsake sin. I have a genuine desire to be with Him. I want to be encircled in the arms of His love. I hope that I can keep that as a goal before me, with enough faith and conviction to keep my sails full, to stay in control, so that I can have a smooth landing in the Kingdom of my Father in Heaven.

On The Cliffs Of Heaven

When Janice and I moved to Carmichael, the first ward activity we went to was a Luau. We didn't know anyone there. After watching Alfred Kaleoonalani Requilman perform his Warrior Dance, Janice leaned over and whispered to me, "I wouldn't want to be caught in a dark alley with him."

A short time later, while sitting in the foyer at Church with a fussy infant, Janice listened to the soothing testimony of this gentle giant. She would have felt comfortable and safe in any situation, with our happy, Warrior of Love.

"Thou shalt live together in love,
insomuch that thou shalt weep for the loss of them that die..."
(D&C 42:45)

In May of 1995, a friend of mine, Kaleo Requilman, was taking time off from his busy schedule to take his family swimming. While the children splashed around in the pool, this thirty-four year old Hawaiian, who was built like a rock, suffered a massive heart attack. He was the last person you would ever expect it to happen to.

His wife Shaunna, rushed him to a nearby hospital where he managed to recover quite well. They kept him in the Intensive Care Unit for testing and observation and said he would be able to go home in a few days. It was during those few days that I had a chance to stay with him so Shaunna could get some rest and spend some time with her four young children.

It was late and visiting hours were long past. Kaleo and I talked about several different things but most of our time was spent talking about his health and how quickly things change. Kaleo worked out at a gym on a regular basis and never even considered himself a candidate for a heart attack. We also talked about high blood pressure and the stress of everyday life. Kaleo told me a story about his childhood, back in the islands of Hawaii and how he used to deal with stress.

Kaleo lived with his family on some cliffs overlooking the mighty Pacific Ocean. When time would permit, often in the early hours of the morning when the waves were breaking clean against a cool offshore breeze, he would stand on the cliffs waxing his favorite surfboard and scan the horizon for waves.

Surfers can save themselves a lot of trouble by studying a break before jumping in and starting to paddle. Knowledge proves greater than brute strength and left only to one's physical ability, the mighty sea will quickly drain the surfer of his energy and take away the very desire to get wet. After making a plan, Kaleo would hit the water with determination and precision timing. His goal was to reach his destination, having fought the least amount of waves, waves that would pound him back toward the cliffs. When he arrived just outside where the waves were breaking, he was not alone. There were others there, friends and acquaintances. This was a beautiful place where they spent valuable time together, sitting on their boards bobbing up and down, all of them sharing a common goal. They were enjoying the beauty of the earth, trying to choose the right wave, one that would take them all the way to shore.

As in life, the big sets didn't always come in. One morning Kaleo would get up early and find that the waves were flat. On another day they might be mushy. Some days the waves weren't any fun at all. Kaleo knew he had to be careful. Even small waves can leave dangerous coral heads exposed, or lurking just below the surface. Sometimes, what seemed like a small mistake could end up a disaster.

The waves were unpredictable and so was life. Waves can close out on you, and send you over the falls for a dangerous ride, pounding you into the bottom. They can send you tumbling beneath the water until you don't know which way is up. You might run out of air before coming up, only to find yourself trying to catch your breath in the two feet of foam left behind by the passing wave.

Sometime during Kaleo's experience, whether on a good day when he was catching every wave, or when he was struggling just to keep his head above the water, he would look up to the cliffs and see his mother waving a white towel high in the air. It was a signal his father and mother set up with him when he was very young. It was a signal to let Kaleo know, it was time to come home.

Our time on Earth is short. How short depends on our perspective. My little girls think a day is forever. If we are going to see their cousins in a few days, they think it will never come. If I tell my daughter we are going in two days she says, "You mean, go to sleep-wake up, go to sleep-wake up, then?" As a youth, I thought four years of high school felt like it took an eternity. Now I'm getting older and time goes so fast I can't keep up with it. I have no doubt we will look back at out visit here on Earth as the blink of the eye.

When I was called to serve as a branch president, the very first call for help that I received was a humbling experience. It happened late at night and within a couple of hours I was in Denver participating in a blessing of the newest member of our branch. Her name was Etana Hager. Her frail little body was lying in an incubator hooked up to a dozen wires and tubes. She was only two days old. The doctors didn't think she was going to make it through the night. Heavenly Father must have had a greater plan for Etana. This precious little baby was only three and a half days old when she went back to be with Heavenly Father.

The other extreme is to live into the golden years. I am reminded of a couple I home taught, Barney and Katie. They were an inspiration to me every time I saw them. When I visited their home, Katie always fussed over treats trying to make me feel welcome. They showed me pictures and told me stories about things and experiences that most people could only read about. I'll never forget conducting a Sacrament Meeting and looking down at those two holding hands like newly-weds. Barney died just before they would have celebrated their seventy-fifth wedding anniversary. He was ninety-four years old. Katie died nine days before her ninety-ninth birthday. Their sojourn on earth was short in the eyes of the Lord, but they managed to accomplish a great deal. There was time for education and for careers. There was time to raise a family and enjoy grandchildren and great-grandchildren.

The fact is, we never know how long we will be here. Every day people die unexpectedly, and everyday people live longer that their doctors predict. My dad has always told me, "You'll never be late when it's your turn to go." Our Creator had the power to give us breath and he surely has the power to take us home when it's time.

Kaleo was doing so well the doctors transferred him out of intensive care and into a regular room. They started talking about when they were going to release him, but once again, Heavenly Father had a different plan. Kaleo suffered another heart attack and never left the hospital alive. It was a sudden and unexpected loss. Those of us who knew him cherish the memories and the times we spent with him.

During the time Kaleo and Shaunna were raising their children, it had been a tradition, that after a long day they would gather around the piano in their living room and sing together. Shaunna and Kaleo both had beautiful voices and they wanted to share that gift with their children. One of the family's favorite songs was *"His Eye Is On The Sparrow."* They loved to sing that one. It was special because Kaleo kept them guessing which part he would sing. He could sing several different harmonies and the challenge was, not to get thrown off when 'Daddy' switched from one part to another.

They also spent a great deal of family time in their front yard. Kaleo and Shaunna would sit in the porch swing, gently rocking and watching their children play. In that swing, they shared confidences, enjoying the sunshine and the outdoors. The porch swing was a symbol of safety and tranquillity in a hectic and sometimes unforgiving world.

The day Kaleo died, I was in their home when Shaunna told her children that their daddy had gone to be with Heavenly Father. I will never forget the Spirit I felt and how Shaunna's testimony gave her the strength to endure such a difficult time. All four of the Requilman children hold a special place in their heart for their dad and one day Whitney, the youngest, was feeling sad as her fourth birthday approached. She was snuggling on the porch swing with her mom, when she confessed, "I hope Heavenly Father will let Daddy come to my birthday party." Shaunna held her tightly.

The morning of Whitney's birthday, Shaunna was hunting for a lost shoe when she noticed a little sparrow on the porch swing that had lost its life. Shaunna brought each of her children out to the porch and held them closely, as they shared a very significant moment. With tears of compassion for the little sparrow, and tears of love for their daddy they quietly considered the words to his favorite song,

Why should I feel discouraged?
Why should the shadows come?
Why should my heart be lonely,
and long for heaven and home?
When Jesus is my portion,
my constant friend is He.
His eye is on the sparrow,
and I know He watches over me.
I sing because I'm happy.
I sing because I'm free.
His eye is on the sparrow,
and I know He watches me.

'His Eye Is On The Sparrow,' by Mrs. S.A. Martin
(© 1994, by Hal Leonard Corporation)

They stood there in silence not knowing what to say, yet knowing that their daddy would surely be in attendance for Whitney's celebration.

As we strive each day as Kaleo did, to live worthy of the opportunities of life on this Earth and enjoy the beauty of God's masterful creation, we are blessed to be a part of his eternal plan. As we bob up and down on the swells of life, we share a common goal, to strive for a perfect ride. As we try to choose all the right waves, please recognize that left to our own strength, the constant buffeting of Satan's destructive waves will wear us down and keep us from our heavenly goal. They will thwart our forward progress and beat us relentlessly into the rocky cliffs of misery.

It is only knowledge, faith and a conviction of our Heavenly Father's plan, and a testimony of the atonement of Christ that will take us safely to our heavenly home. No matter what ocean we are on, or how strong the currents are that we fight, if we continue to paddle in the right direction, one day we will see that white towel waving high upon the cliffs of heaven as Kaleo did. And we will be ready to accept the call to come home.

This Mud's For You?

Addiction can be a horrible way of life.

In the deaf community, a natural question directed toward an interpreter is, "What got you interested in Sign Language?" When I made a commitment to live the Word of Wisdom, I had more than twelve hours a day to find something else to do. I went to the library and picked up a book called, The Joy of Signing. The answer I give to my deaf friends is always the same. I used Sign Language as a crutch. I replaced some bad habits with a good one.

"And [you] shall run and not be weary, and shall walk and not faint."
(D&C 89:20)

I left the faucet on while alternately running my hands through the water and over my head. This primitive, 'wet-finger' combing technique has tamed many a bad hair day for me. I noticed my hair was getting a little thin on top, and my hair-line was receding. For a moment, the man looking back at me from the mirror was my father. He used to comb his hair exactly the same way.

I started thinking, I haven't used a brush or comb in years. I remember as a kid, hearing my Dad threaten to chain a brush to the vanity in the bathroom. I have four sisters and it seemed like no matter how many combs and brushes dad bought, there was never one around when he needed it. Now, decades later, with six daughters of my own, I wonder if I have adapted to the 'wet-finger comb' out of necessity, or if it has been genetically passed down from my ancestors?

Mankind, is continually adapting to different situations, stimuli, and the changing environmental forces that surround us. For example, as I get older I have become more patient. At the same time, I am less willing to fight the bitter cold and high altitude of my Colorado home. I am changing, adapting mentally and physically every day to the world around me. Some things change quickly and others, so slowly that I don't even realize it's happening.

I would like to address some of the changes that we force upon our bodies even when our bodies make it crystal clear from the very beginning that the changes are bad.

I was sitting on a beach in Mexico the first time I was offered a taste of beer from an adult. I almost retched trying to swallow it. It was without a doubt the most foul taste that I had ever experienced. But as disgusting as it was, I will also never forget what an honor it was to be treated like a grown up for the first time. When I was a kid, it wasn't so much that beer was bad for you, but everybody knew beer was only for grownups. Being offered a drink made me feel like I had come of age. I felt an immediate change. It was like breaking through the chrysalis of my youth and metamorphorizing into an adult. It was a privilege. I couldn't wait to gloat over my older sisters. "You'll never guess, I just drank a beer on the beach!"

If beer were really such a great thing, why did it taste so terrible? And why did my body want to reject it? Imagine anyone drinking a shot of hard alcohol for the very first time and not hating it. It burns like crazy (which is a good sign it doesn't belong on the inside of the body). Most people gasp and cough from the effect alcohol has on them and by the end of that first experience they usually end up on their knees, worshipping at the white porcelain alter. It seems clear to me, that if the taste of alcohol was the only thrill of drinking, age limits wouldn't be necessary to prevent children from using it. The problem is, there are many other things influencing people to drink. The people who manufacture alcoholic beverages consider it a success when anyone manages to develop a tolerance for the taste of alcohol and graduate to needing it.

I was in Boulder, Colorado when once again I found myself trying to be more like 'the grown ups.' I got my hands on a cigarette and headed out behind the haystack with a friend. It was my first try at smoking. I feel relatively confident in making the statement that every single person who has ever tried smoking has had the same first reaction. You light up one of the little cancer sticks, take a puff of the toxic, smoldering, nicotine delivery device, and breathe its billowing death into your perfect pink lungs. There's really only one possible reaction your body can have, a heaving rejection. Yours truly, behind the hay-stack, violently hacked from the very center of my being. Peering through a cloud of smoke I managed to choke out a, "mmm... these are good." I was trying not to show my true feelings about the experience and what I was thinking, which was, *Maybe I'm not quite mature enough for these yet.* It didn't look all that natural to have a cigarette balanced between my fingers, at least not as natural as it did for those people on television.

The reality is, all of these debilitating substances, cigarettes, alcohol, and illicit drugs are tools used by Satan, *"for he seeketh that all men might be miserable like unto himself." (2 Nephi 2:27)* It amazes me how Satan can take activities that can only bring sorrow and destruction, and convince us that participating in them will make us look cool, more popular, and increase our stature. We are so gullible. We must be so easy to convince, to pursued. Our bodies are temples wherein the Holy Ghost can dwell. How then can we fall for the marketing strategies of the evil one. He wants only to *"drag [us] down to the gulf of misery and endless wo..." (Helaman 5:12)*

The resilience of the human body is nothing short of miraculous. It has baffled doctors and scientists for centuries. That miracle is the body's ability to heal itself and to adapt to so many different conditions. The thing that concerns me, is how easily our bodies adapt to and becomes comfortable with the negative influences that bombard us.

Too often we ignore our body when it warns us. In my examples, the warnings were not subtle. It wasn't a, *Gee, I'm not sure if we should be doing this*. It was a crystal clear rejection. More like, *If you take one more drink of that, I'm going to show you the inside of your stomach.* Or, *If you take one more puff of that, you're going to cough up a lung.*

The sad part of this metamorphosis between rejecting of harmful substances and embracing them is, that along the way we have had to ignore the warnings and force these substances into our systems. Often because we are trying to be mature, accepted, or grown up. We are only fooling ourselves. We literally have to cram these transgression down our throats to become comfortable with them. The worst part of it is how, over time, our bodies adapt to these things. An experimental drinker that continues to quaff down the nasty tasting gruel, eventually acquires a taste for it. It starts to tastes good to him and the clincher is when his body goes the extra mile and develops a need for it, an addiction. When the addiction becomes so strong, that we would rather die, than live without it, *"The devil laugheth, and his angels rejoice..." (3 Nephi 9:2.)* How we can adapt to such deadly habits? It makes no sense.

For the smoker it's the same thing. If he continues to puff on those nasty cancer sticks long enough, he will eventually be able to inhale the smoke without hacking. In fact, he will develop a taste for them and eventually a need for them. Cigarettes have been compared to heroin when it comes to the difficult task of 'kicking the habit.' Another devastating problem associated with drug abuse is that of peer pressure.

I was twelve years old when I was convinced to take a little white pill before school. Our family had just moved to Southern California, and it was my first day going to a new school. I was told that if I took that pill it would help me be more talkative and outgoing. *If you knew me, that would be funny.* I took the pill, and I think I met every student and faculty member at Einstein Junior High in one day. Humorous? No. For the next twelve years I would experiment with every kind of drug under the sun.

I didn't start out by sticking needles in my arm, but when I let people convince me that a little speed was okay, or marijuana, I was headed in that direction. At first I made comments like, "I'll smoke pot, but I would never do psychedelic drugs. Those are bad for you." But when I started hanging around with people who used them, I joined in. The closer I got to a new kind of drug, the less dangerous it seemed. From the psychedelics I looked at the people who were using needles and used the same words again, "I'd never do that, they're crazy." But associating with them made it seem less threatening. Twelve years is a long time to abuse your body with harmful drugs. From the time you wake up in the morning until you crash at night is a great deal of time to waste. The cost involved in supporting a drug habit can get astronomical, and many users become involved in selling drugs.

When I decided to quit using drugs, I was a saxophone player in a rock band. We traveled around Colorado and Wyoming playing in all of the ski towns, skiing all day, and playing music all night. It sounds like fun, and I would be lying if I said none of it was. But let me put it into perspective.

It was two-thirty in the morning and we just finished playing in Keystone, Colorado. The bouncers cleared all of the people out of the club and locked the doors. The bartender invited the band up to the bar for the traditional after hours drinks. My bass player, who was like a brother to me, fell off his barstool because he was so drunk. We all laughed hysterically and helped him back onto his stool. We said, "What's the matter Bruce? Come on, have another one!"

About two months later, we were back at The Snake River Saloon. It was the same bar, the same time of the morning, and the same barstool. Like a replay, Bruce fell off his barstool again. This time I wasn't sitting at the bar with them. I was rolling up microphone cords on the stage, watching what was happening at the bar. They were laughing again, but I cried.

The difference in my attitude was the fact that I was straight. I was about a week away from being baptized, and I was trying to live the Word of Wisdom. I played in the band for five and a half months after I joined the Church. Before it seemed like fun to be on stage, looking out over a night club full of people partying and getting crazy. But the reason it looked like fun was because I was just as loaded as they were. Probably worse. Standing on stage when I was straight was completely different. I saw people who were trying to forget reality. Instead of trying to find themselves, they were trying to lose themselves.

To understand how your perspective changes when you use drugs, one only needs to look at the adjectives drugs-users prefer to use, when they refer to what it is they do; "Let's get small, messed up, stupid, ripped, stoned, trashed, and wasted." In my opinion, none of those words represent an activity that could be mistaken for something good.

I am convinced that the human body can and will adapt to almost anything. If it can take a healthy functioning lung, designed to operate on oxygen, and adapt to craving foul carcinogenic fumes, I think the body can do anything, anything at all.

For example; I believe if you were to walk out in your back yard and dig up a tea spoon of dirt and try to eat it, you probably wouldn't like it. Your body might even try to reject it. You might have a hard time getting the first few spoonfuls down...BUT, if eating dirt was cool, and everyone who was anyone was eating dirt, you might try a little harder. If you knew that if your friends could see you putting away a teaspoon or two, you'd be a "happen'n dude", you might just force a little down. You might spit some of it out at first, but if you spent enough time in your garden munchin', I believe you would eventually develop a taste for it. If you kept it up long enough, who knows, your body might even develop a need for it.

I'm not completely crazy. I realize that marketing plays a huge part in the promotion of substance abuse. It's a major part of the hype that drives these products of destruction. Satan has a skilled team of advertisers who do their best to camouflage the products that kill. They try to make them look attractive, fun, prestigious, safe, cool. If we wanted to give the 'dirt' campaign a fair try, we would have to develop a plan to promote it. We'd have to give it some pizzazz, if for no other reason than to get people past the first spoonful.

First, we would need to choose a mascot. Not a camel, but maybe we could use a worm or a mole. And it would have to be cute so that kids will like it. The sooner we could get them dirty the better. If we made the mascot hip enough, everyone would want to have a picture of it on their hat, or coat. We could sponsor some sporting activities, throw money in the direction of politicians. We could create an association between eating dirt and having a better lifestyle. "It improves your complexion, makes you more attractive." I think the public would buy it. We would have to convince people that eating dirt will attract men to women and vice versa. It has to freshen your breath or make your teeth brighter (that might be a stretch).

Let's not forget the importance of packaging. We could put dirt in a can that would fit snugly in the back pocket of a pair of jeans, or in a pack that fits comfortably in the front pocket of a shirt. It would have to be something that people could get used to having with them every waking hour of the day.

Variety is important. We could develop different brands of dirt. Give people a choice. That's good marketing. We could offer, Red Clay, Black Soil, and Shale Mini's. We could open up stylish franchises like those yuppie coffee shops. We could make a really powerful mud drink in espresso-like machines and people everywhere will go nuts over it. We can create an atmosphere that brings people together.

Some people will be concerned about the extra weight a two pack-a-day dirt habit can put on you. We'll have to develop some light products like, dust, or even mud light. I can see the billboards now. Marty Mole, leaning against a silver Jaguar, surrounded by scantly clad super models. The caption reads, "This Mud's For You."

But seriously, our bodies are incredible. It's true they will adapt in many ways, but they are better suited to adapt to positive stimulus. Twelve years of my life were wasted on substance abuse. It was a waste of twelve good years. I can only wonder how much healthier I would be if I hadn't put my body through so much abuse. Think of all the brain cells I must have destroyed.

I've had seventeen years to recover from the adverse effects of drugs. I'm thankful for the adaptability of the human body, and how it is working in a positive way for me right now. The journey from a grain of sand on the tip of your tongue, to putting away an acre of rich Kansas farmland, is an ugly road to travel. Don't believe in the marketing. Don't believe the destroyer. No matter how fun it looks on the outside, it is a life filled with pain and misery. Save your brain-cells. I promise you it's not worth it. If you have already been doing some excavating, if there's dirt under your fingernails, it's not too late to stop. Today is the day. If I can do it, anyone can.

"Come now, and let us reason together, saith the Lord: though your sins be as scarlet, they shall be as white as snow; though they be red like crimson, they shall be as wool."
(Isaiah 1:18)

Achieve Your Goals

A New Year's Resolution

"...but thou shalt meditate therin day and night, that thou mayest observe to do according to all that is written therin: for then thou shalt make thy way prosperous, and then thou shalt have good success.
(Joshua 1:8)

Achieve Your Goals

Bear with me a while, I'd like to discuss,
some things that are personal, so just between us.
I'm sure you've experienced, some goals not achieved,
yet when you set them, you whole heartedly believed.
I'll study my scriptures, I'll get out of bed,
I won't allow bad thoughts, into my head.
I'll work out, I'll lose weight, I'll be thankful, not moan,
I might even commit, to spend more time at home.
But each time that you start, and don't follow through,
there's something that happens, down inside of you.
Some even get used to, the idea of "I can't,"
and others become livid, they rave and they rant!
I could have, I should have, I didn't, I'll never,
these feeling could haunt us for ever and ever.
So remember it's Satan, who loves to depress,
and the Savior who comforts, and takes away stress.
Whatever the reason, you fell short of your plan,
pick yourself back up, and do the best that you can.
Now let's change our focus, to the goals that we met,
achieved by persistence, or because of a bet.
I danced at the dance, or I passed my test,
I gave a talk, and it felt like my best.
I won the race, or I made the team,
have you got the picture, do you know what I mean?
Regardless of size, monumental or small,
that feeling of success, is a comfort to all.
If we'd spend more of our time, and think positive,
we'd reap the blessings, and change how we live.
The world will look brighter, and we'll do our best,
with a smile on our face, and our chin off our chest.
So if I could give you, one last piece of advice,
if you'll trust me on this one, it's going to be nice.
Remember there's nothing outside your reach to do,
just say I can, I will, and then follow through.

A Heart For Service

I came home from work in the middle of the day. I ran in the house and Janice was sitting on the couch in her bath robe. She asked why I was home so early. I said, "Hurry, get some clothes on we have company." When she asked who it was, I said it was a surprise and that she wouldn't believe me if I told her. I almost pushed her down the hall to go get ready. When she came back into the room, there was a black man sitting on our couch with his suit coat pulled up over his head. "Guess who I am?" he said. "Guess who I am?" I was laughing my head off and Janice was less than amused. When the joke was up, I told her, "Put it this way, you wouldn't want to get caught in the ring with him." It was Muhammad Ali.

Later, in 1984, The Champ invited me to his home in Los Angeles after a day at the Olympics. After a private showing of his favorite magic tricks, he autographed a poster for me. It says,
"Service to others is the rent we pay for our room in Heaven."

"...when ye are in the service of your fellow beings
ye are only in the service of your God."
(Mosiah 2:17)

I was visiting a stake Primary leadership meeting one Sunday to set apart our new Primary nursery leader, Denece Zavoral. I was the only priesthood holder in the meeting, so I stepped into the hallway of the church to find someone to assist me in setting her apart. The very first priesthood holder that walked by was Bill Wright, the Young Men president of one of our wards. He was hurrying off to a meeting when I asked him if he could take a few minutes and assist me. He was happy to help.

Bill and I went back into the meeting, and while Denece sat in a chair, we placed our hands on her head and closed our eyes. Everyone in the room stopped talking and a quiet reverence fell over the group. I listened for the Spirit of inspiration and proceeded to give Denece a blessing. It wasn't long before I realized there was a ticking sound beating out the rhythm of my words. It was brother Wright's heart.

When Bill Wright was a young man, he had a valve replaced in his heart. The doctors used a pig's valve that would only last about ten years. When it needed replacing they repeated the process. He recently hit the twenty year mark and went in for his third operation. Technology is such that this time they installed a mechanical valve that they claim will last the rest of his life. Bill is excited to think that he will not have to endure another heart surgery, but his wife says that the ticking of his new valve keeps her awake at night.

While I was giving Denece the blessing, I was overcome with emotion. I wondered if it was a coincidence that Bill was standing next to me. I wasn't surprised that he had been so eager to help me when I asked. Good people are like that. The beating of his heart was the perfect music to accompany Denece's blessing. She, too, had a heart for service.

When our stake Primary president presented me with Denece's name as her recommendation for a new Stake Primary Nursery Leader, she told me that she had prayed about it and felt inspired that Denece was the person the Lord wanted for the calling. She also told me that she was aware that Denece was pregnant and was having some health complications. She told me that she was more than willing to wait until the baby was born and Denece was feeling better before she would give Denece any assignments.

The process of approving Denece for the calling started when I presented her name in my stake presidency meeting. My stake president knew far more than I did about Denece's situation and initially didn't think she would be able to handle the calling because of her health. But after prayer and consideration, it was decided that I should discuss the idea with her husband, Gary. From Gary, to her bishop, and to her father who was on the High Council, everyone had a dozen reasons why she couldn't do the calling, but no one wanted to tell me that our stake Primary president wasn't inspired when she submitted the name. It was time to ask Denece.

I have extended a fair number of callings since I have been a member of the Church. I have had more than one qualified and able person turn down a calling, sometimes for reasons I didn't understand. Walking up to Denece's house, I expected to be turned down. During that interview I learned what courage Nephi had when he accepted the overwhelming assignment of obtaining the brass plates from Laban. He said, *"...I will go and do the things which the Lord hath commanded..." (1 Nephi 3:7)*

Denece Zavoral was born in February of 1961. The doctors said she was a perfect little baby and both mother and daughter were sent home with a clean bill of health. A day or two later, her dad was playing with her on the floor when he heard what sounded like the 'whoosh, whoosh' of water being forced through a garden hose. Denece claims, "That's when they took me back to the hospital for a refund!"

The doctors were surprised to have missed such a loud murmur, and immediately set up an appointment with a specialist. She was a 'blue baby'. The doctor said she would not survive more than a year and warned her parents not to get too attached. At that time the technology was not available to do anything about it. The doctors told them that any emotional flare-up would increase the stress on her tiny heart. They were to try and keep her from crying. When she did, she turned blue. One day, as hard as they tried to keep her calm, she started to cry. To their surprise, she didn't turn blue. It was the first positive sign that she might live.

When Denece was four years old, she had her first heart-catheterization. It was a success but they discovered a medium, to small size hole in her heart. The doctors said there was slight possibility the hole might grow shut on its own. But they couldn't understand why they had been convinced for so long that the hole was much larger.

Denece grew up, and other than running out of breath quicker than the other kids, she participated in most activities. If she were too aggressive, she still turned blue. At fourteen, she went in for another heart-catheterization and the results were basically the same. It was shortly after that evaluation when her doctor told her she would never be able to bear children. The stress and strain of childbirth would be too much for her heart. He told her that trying to have a baby would probably kill her. She was devastated.

When Denece was nineteen she fell in love with Gary, and they decided to get married. She wanted to have one more heart-catheterization before the wedding to see how things were progressing with her heart. There were still problems. Blood that was already oxygenated was washing back and mixing with blood that had not been oxygenated. Her heart was working over-time. This wasn't a good sign, but because it wasn't mixing the other way around, and because of Denece's strong desire to have a baby, the doctors told her to go ahead and try. "Let's see what happens," they said.

Denece married Gary, and like clockwork they were blessed with a baby girl. And then another. Everything was going according to plan. Their children were healthy. During the seventh month of her third pregnancy, Denece's lips and finger tips started turning blue. She felt fine, but her doctor told her to stop working anyway. Baby number three was born and everyone was happy. Her fourth pregnancy was about the same. As long as she took it easy during the last trimester, she had healthy babies.

It was after her fourth baby that she didn't bounce back like she should have. She was tired all the time and getting slower at accomplishing anything. At first she blamed it on the extra pounds she was carrying after the pregnancy and the fact that she was getting older. There was also the possibility that keeping up with four children had something to do with it. She said, "I thought everyone had to stop and rest in the middle of vacuuming." But the reality was, her physical condition had been deteriorating for years.

By this time Denece was thirty years old. She was working at a hospital with heart patients, an environment she grew up in. Denece was exhausted. "I felt like I was going to die," she said. "I still remember sitting on the couch and calling my mom. I didn't tell her how I felt, I just wanted to hear her voice before it was over. I kept thinking, this is it. I'm going to die. This will be the last time I talk to my mom." After she hung up the phone, she called Gary and told him how serious her condition was. Denece went to her primary care physician who failed to see her real problem. He tried blaming how she felt on everything from the salt in her diet, to her age. She refused to accept his diagnosis. "I'm thirty, not a hundred!" she said. He finally gave her some medication to take off some of the water she was retaining, if for no other reason than her insistence. When she mentioned the episode to one of the doctors she worked with, he scheduled her in for an immediate heart-cath. Within two weeks, Denece was having open heart surgery.

What the doctors found was nothing short of a miracle. Sometime between when she was born and her fourth birthday, her Tricuspid valve fell apart. One of the three leaflets (flaps) swung down and re-attached itself to the heart. The amazing thing was, it covered the original hole that had threatened her life as an infant.

During her first heart-cath at the age of four, the medium to small size hole the doctors had found, was only a small portion of the original hole. It was the part that the 'self patch' had failed to cover. That 'self patch' had kept her alive well beyond the one year the doctors gave her to live, and for that matter, it was the 'self patch' that allowed her to have any children at all.

The doctor repaired her tricuspid valve using plastic parts, a small ring and what was left of the original valve. During the operation her AV node was damaged. It sends an electrical signal to the lower part of the heart and causes it to beat. Because hers was not working, she required the use of a temporary pace-maker.

Every once in a while just to see if Denece's AV node was going to start working again on its own, the doctor would disconnect her pace-maker. "I could see my heart beating on the monitor and listen to the beep, beep, beep. After a few seconds, the beep stopped and the line went flat. That's when I passed out, and the doctor turned the pace-maker back on. If he didn't, I would have died." This unpleasant ritual went on a couple times a day until they decided to install a permanent pace-maker. The best part was, she was alive. And all she needed to do was put in a new battery every ten years. But things never really bounced back all the way. The cardiologist had some theories. One may have been her body's reaction to the pace-maker, also there may have been too much prior damage to her heart. The bottom line was, from years of punching blood back the wrong way, her heart was like a rubber band that had been stretched too many times. It wouldn't pump right. Her blood didn't flow fast enough to remove water from her body and she was continually building up fluids. They tried different things to solve the problem, but medication was the only thing that helped. Since that time, Denece has had to take medication every day to keep from retaining fluids and to help reduce heart rhythm problems. Because of those medications, once again she was told she would not be able to have any more children. Gary and Denece were thankful enough to have four children already, but they remembered a distinct impression Gary had after their fourth child was born. He told Denece that he felt certain they were going to have a fifth child. Referring to his feeling Denece said, "No, I don't think so." By the end of the discussion it ended up as a joke, and they never talked about it again.

Five years later, Denece thought she was pregnant. The first thing she did was go to her cardiologist. His exact words were, "I don't think so. There is no way you can be on this kind of medication and carry a baby. You can't be doing this." Next, she went to her obstetrician who confirmed her feelings. She was definitely pregnant. He told her not to get too comfortable with the idea because he didn't feel the pregnancy would be allowed to run its course.

Before Denece and Gary told anyone about the pregnancy, they went to see their stake president. They asked him to give her a priesthood blessing. In the blessing, Denece was told that her baby was a very special child, and that she would be able to carry the baby to full term. She was told that her heart would endure all the pressures and problems associated with the pregnancy, and that the baby would be 'perfect in every way.' Not healthy, not cute (with a full head of hair,) but perfect in every way. After the blessing she went back to her doctor and told him that she planned to go against his advice and give the baby every chance to live.

The decision to go forward with the pregnancy meant that she would have to stop taking her medication for the first trimester. If she managed to make it that far without losing the baby, her doctors would re-evaluate her condition and determine if her heart was going to be strong enough for the remaining six months.

In the four previous years, under the strict observation of her doctor, Denece tried more than once to stop taking her medication. Every time the answer was the same. She would never be able to survive without them.

The doctors were not happy with her decision to carry the baby and advised her against it. But Denece could not forget the words of her blessing, and her faith was strong enough that she expected every word of it to be true.

What surprised the doctors more than her commitment to carry the baby, was her health during that first three months. She refused to take her medicine and not only did she not die, but she felt better than she had for years. At twelve weeks exactly, she started retaining water and had to go back on her medication. The doctors remained skeptical with a 'wait-and-see' attitude.

Denece went in for ultrasounds every week to monitor the baby's progress. One time Denece and Gary remember the doctor telling them, "The baby is alive now, but by twenty weeks I'm sure we'll have to take it. Don't get too attached." That day when they walked out of the doctor's office, Denece told Gary, "If it hadn't been for my blessing, I would be devastated by what he just said." The blessing was on her mind every step of the way. "It was my only hope," she said.

Back on her medication, the pregnancy progressed, but Denece's health was getting worse. At five months she couldn't even walk to the car. She struggled to breath. Her body wasn't getting enough oxygen. When her doctor found out how she was feeling, he told her to stay down. If she was going anywhere, it would have to be in a wheelchair.

Physically she was a wreck. Her lips and fingertips were blue most of the time. She felt as though she was going to suffocate. There were lots of times when she wanted to give up. It was more than she could handle. She probably would have quit, if it hadn't been for the promises of the blessing.

Five perinatologists met to discuss her situation. They felt that continuing the pregnancy would result in Denece suffering permanent heart damage. Their recommendation was to take the baby immediately. She was twenty weeks into the pregnancy and Denece asked what the chances were of the baby surviving. They told her minimal at best. Denece looked the doctors right in the eye and said, "But I've had a blessing, and the baby is going to be fine. I have faith, and I'm going to have a healthy baby."

The doctors reacted sarcastically, but just to pacify their patient they ordered another echo-cardiogram. If this test was bad, they would stick with their recommendation to terminate the pregnancy. Once again the doctors were amazed. The test results were perfect. Her blood tests came out crazy, her oxygen levels were messed up, but the results of the echo were indicative of a healthy heart. The doctor said, "They must have messed up the echo."

Denece was confused. On one hand she was upset that the echo didn't explain why she felt so bad, and on the other hand she was devastated by the reality of it all. If that test had not been perfect, she might have caved in under the pressure and let them take her baby. The thought of it still haunts her.

The team of doctors met again and decided to give her two more weeks. Then they would do another echo. It was perfect again, and again, and again. Her health was deteriorating. She was a wreck. She was restricted to total bed rest and unable to do almost anything for herself. Because of the test results, the doctors really couldn't say much more about ending the pregnancy, but they were sure of one thing, they were going to take the baby early. The smaller the baby was for the delivery, the less stress it would put on Denece's heart. At that point the goal was to take the baby six weeks early.

It was about that time that I walked up to Denece's house, anticipating that she would decline the call to serve in the stake Primary. I was totally unprepared for the experience I was about to have. She was sitting on the couch during our interview, but probably wished she were still in bed. She filled me in on how wonderful her ward had been, and how they never stopped bringing food and helping with her children. They even helped clean her house. She was gracious and credited her ward family as one of the reasons she had made it so far. It was in that interview that she first told me about the blessing she received from our stake president. I've never met anyone who took a blessing more literally than she did. She knew her baby was going to be healthy and that was that.

I asked Denece if she would accept the calling and told her that the stake Primary president and I knew it would be a while before she could start serving. I told her that after the baby was born and after she felt better I would set her apart. She never considered declining the call. I was shocked.

For two weeks the doctors injected her with steroids in an effort to speed up the development of the baby's lungs. The unfortunate side effect was an increase of stress on Denece's heart. When the time arrived to take the baby (early), they did an amniocentesis and found that the baby's lungs were not yet fully developed. Denece was frustrated again. She was looking forward to the delivery. "I was tired of being pregnant and all-together sick. I was tired of the tests and the doctors. I hated to be dependent on everyone," she said.

For two more weeks she was stuck in bed waiting. The next date scheduled to take the baby would have been four weeks early. Denece and

Gary packed a bag and headed for the hospital. When they got there, they found out that their new insurance company refused to cover the delivery without another amnio. They wanted proof that the baby was healthy. If it wasn't, they would have to deliver at a different hospital. Reluctantly they did the amnio and the baby's lungs were still not developed enough. Denece was getting mad. She was ready to get that baby out. She was even starting to get mad at herself for having so much faith in the blessing, "The heck with full term," she said. She was ready to have the baby.

If you believe in Murphy's Law, that anything that can go wrong will go wrong, you won't be shocked at what happened next. Denece was home in bed, like always, when she got a phone call from one of her sons. "Dad's dead on the basketball court!" he shouted. This wasn't funny to Denece who had administered CPR on a man who died of a heart attack on that same basketball court one year before. What her son really meant was, in the middle of a game, Gary had crashed to the floor in pain with a hurt leg. Denece told her son, "Yea right, tell your dad to get home, I need him to put the little kids to bed."

Gary was in surgery the following day and Denece was furious with him. It was bad enough that they were dependent on their parents and friends to bring in food, and care for the children while Gary was at work. But now with both of them stuck in bed, it was more than she could handle.

By the time she actually went in for the delivery, it was almost comical. The hospital staff had been anticipating her delivery for so long it was a standing joke. They had run mock deliveries to choreograph the events that needed to take place. There would be so many doctors and nurses in the room because of the possibility of her heart giving out during the delivery that everything had to be coordinated. There was one other problem, how were they going to fit Gary into the picture? He insisted on being present for the delivery, even if he would have to be on crutches. The labor and delivery went routinely. Denece wasn't surprised that during most of her labor, Gary was comfortably snoring away in the other bed.

Denece is currently serving as the Stake Primary Nursery Leader and serving with the same kind of faith and enthusiasm she had when she accepted the call, with faith in every heartbeat. And the baby? Matthew was a perfect, healthy eight pound, seven ounce boy. And why not? Just because Denece was told she could never have children, and because everything that could go wrong, did? Looking back on everything that happened, Denece still draws strength from the blessing she received. "I just kept hearing it over and over in my mind, 'Healthy in every way,' and I knew it would work out fine."

Whether we are asked to help a friend on the spur of the moment like Brother Wright was, or called by inspiration as Sister Zavoral was, the decision to serve is only difficult if we make it that way. We can usually think up a dozen reasons why we can't, and there may be others around us who might agree. But the real decision comes down to one thing, your heart.

"...serve the Lord thy God with all thy heart and with all thy soul,..."
(Deuteronomy 10:12)

Chumline

"...there is an opposition in all things..." (2 Nephi 2:11) Heavenly Father is loving and compassionate. He wants us to enjoy eternal happiness and through His prophets He teaches, "...whatsoever thing persuadeth men to do good is of me; for good cometh of none save it be of me..." (Ether 4:12)

Just as beautiful as life can be when we follow the Savior, it can get ugly if we follow the enticements of the devil.

I haven't gone hunting or shark fishing in more than nine years, and I agree with my wife, 'Chumline' is a little bit graphic for some readers. I decided to leave it in Cheap Sunglasses, because of the way it illustrates the "cunning plan of the evil one!" (2 Nephi 9:28) After reading it you will probably do one of two things; call the Fish and Game and send me a letter of reprimand or you'll order a shark steak the next time you go to a nice restaurant.

"...that he might lead away the souls of men down to hell–yea, that great pit which hath been digged for the destruction of men..." (1 Nephi 14:3)

For my brother and I, a successful shark hunt in Catalina begins early in the morning with the rattle of an alarm clock in Long Beach, California. After stopping at an all night grocery store to buy cat food, we put the boat into the water and negotiated the long channel that would take us beyond the marina and out to sea.

After clearing the breakwater, we set a course for the bait barge where, for a small fee and listening to a big fish story from the old man who works there, we would buy a half-scoop of anchovies. Then it was "Catalina, here we come."

By the time we passed the off-shore oil rigs, we could always find a school of mackerel churning up the phosphorescent water in an effort to escape from a larger fish. With light tackle and using the anchovies for bait, we would cast into the boil and pull out a mackerel every time. When we took the mackerel off our hooks, we cut them in half and dropped them into five-gallon buckets. Mackerel are an especially bloody fish and when you add them to a couple gallons of sea-water, they make a great bucket of chum.

By then we would be singing at the top of our lungs, "Twenty-six miles across the sea, Santa Catalina's got a shark for me!" And if the weather cooperated, it would be another successful day of shark fishing.

Floating off the south tip of the island with our engines off and the barking of sea lions echoing across the water, we started the slow, yet productive process of setting a chumline. If we were patient and consistent, we would catch our limit of sharks.

We filled a wire basket with mackerel halves and lowered it off the stern just below the surface of the water. After pouring a little blood into the water, we set up two fishing poles with large hooks and baited them with mackerel halves. We tossed them in and let them drift about forty feet behind the boat. Now there was nothing left to do but watch the seagulls and relax in the sunshine. Inevitably, some unsuspecting shark swimming around in the clear blue water would cross our chumline. The shark's natural curiosity and quest for food would almost always turn them in the direction of the boat. They would get all worked up in a feeding frenzy, assuming they were on the trail of a wounded fish. When they got close enough and could see what they thought was a helpless mackerel drifting behind the boat, they attacked every time.

There are a few elements that can make a shark hunt more productive. The first is to occasionally flick some cat food into the water. The oily cat food has a strong scent and sharks can't resist it! Another important element is the weather. Imagine a chumline of fish guts, blood, and cat food drifting behind the boat on a calm day. It's an enticing trap for any shark that comes near, but if the boat sits in one place, a shark would have to swim right up to it in order to detect the chum. On the other hand, if you had a nice steady breeze, the boat would drift for miles and miles, leaving a long trail of chum behind it. On the ideal day, a shark swimming in any direction for miles around, would have a good chance of crossing the chumline. When it did, there was a strong possibility it would change directions and follow the trail of chum.

After the shark hit the bait and I tried to jerk its teeth out setting the hook, the shark still didn't always know it was hooked. They were usually so focused on satisfying their appetites, they didn't pay much attention to the pain of the hook. Although I could be pulling and reeling with all my strength, most sharks never really fought back until they saw the bottom of the boat. Only then would they turn away and dive. They used their razor sharp teeth to try and cut the line, but we had stainless steel leaders to prevent that. The sharks would twist and turn, trying everything they could to spit out the hook. But if we kept the line tight, they couldn't get away. Eventually, the shark would give up, and if I managed to pull it close enough to the boat, my brother would gaff it with a long pole that had a huge hook on the end and we would have our shark.

Sharks are extremely strong. Their skin is like armor, and if they break teeth off during an attack, they have several rows ready to roll forward and replace the broken ones. I'm convinced if you threw a shark back into the water after you cleaned it, it would still try to swim away. I wonder, if they are so tough and well equipped for their environment, why are they so easy to catch?

Not unlike the sharks, everyday we swim through the crystal blue waters of life. Day after day we are exposed to the filthy chumlines Satan has patiently set to entice us into following his boat. Satan is a skilled fisher, and occasionally flicks a little temptation in our direction. His goal is to work us into a frenzy. Too often we are so focused on the stream of filth surrounding him that we can't see clearly. Then we take the bait. How often do we deny being hooked until we see the bottom of the boat? By then, spitting the hook is no easy task. We dive and pull away, but are often reeled back in. We are faced with a serious choice. We can either escape to freedom and life, or let Satan wear us down, reel us in, and destroy us.

We were created by the same God who desires us to be happy. *"There hath no temptation taken you but such as is common to man: but God [is] faithful, who will not suffer you to be tempted above that ye are able; but will with the temptation also make a way to escape, that ye may be able to bear [it.]" (1 Corinthians 10:13)* Heavenly Father made us strong and well equipped for our environment. Like the shark we must fight back, and avoid destruction.

Whatever oceans you find yourself swimming in, regardless of where you come from or where you are going, if you cross a chumline that smells of trouble, keep right on swimming.

The Thing

I wasn't born so long ago that students in Middle School weren't involved with sex, but back then it wasn't talked about openly. People referred to sex more like, you know, "the thing."

"...whatsoever thing persuadeth men to do evil,
...ye may know with a perfect knowledge it is of the devil..."
(Moroni 7:17)

Some friends of mine and I left Colorado on a business trip to Tucson, Arizona. In an effort to stay on course, we regularly checked our road map. It was terribly hot, and this wasn't any place to make a wrong turn. It didn't take long before the stretches of desert highway became boring, and my mind started to wander. Instead of having my destination clearly in mind, I started staring into the open desert and daydreaming.

Just when I thought I'd go nuts from the endless sand and cactus, I noticed a sign on the horizon. When we got closer, I realized it wasn't a sign; it was a gigantic billboard. The only words written on it were, "The Thing." It didn't mention the name of a town, an exit number or anything. It was obvious that someone had spent a small fortune to construct that billboard way out there in the middle of the desert. In my opinion, the billboard was a waste of money. There was nothing else to look at out there but desert, and I would have paid just as much attention to a bumper sticker on a mile marker.

About the time my friends and I quit talking about the oddity of the billboard, up popped another one. This one didn't offer much more information about what "The Thing" was. It was only another tease, clearly designed to build anticipation. The person responsible for the billboard had one thing in mind. His goal is to entice travelers, to spend their precious vacation dollars, and to make himself rich.

If you have ever driven across Nevada, between Sacramento and Salt Lake City, you have undoubtedly seen the billboards that advertise the city of Winnemucca. Some are silly, some stupid, but all are designed to create interest. They are designed to start you thinking about it. By repeated enticements, you become curious. The billboards in Arizona were a lot like those for Winnemucca. My friends and I discussed the marketing strategy of the advertiser, and understood how this style of advertising could be successful. After all, being intelligent businessmen, we were far too smart to fall for this kind of scam. Let's face it, if they had something really worthwhile to advertise, for example, a Big Mac, a small Golden Arches decal stapled to a cactus would have been sufficient.

For the next sixty miles or so, there was one billboard after another, and this "Thing" was becoming more and more the topic of our conversation. After all, some of the ads were funny, and that made us spend more and more time talking about it. We even started making our own jokes about it.

When we finally arrived at the exit marked "The Thing", even though we had previously decided not to, we found ourselves caught up in the flow of traffic and followed everyone else at the turn-off. It looked like everyone was headed in the same direction. Even as we exited the freeway, my friends and I agreed not to waste our money on the "Thing." All we needed was gas and drinks, and this was as good a place as any.

When we went inside the store to pay for the gas, there in the back corner of the store was a gate marked "The Thing." It didn't surprise me that in order to experience this "Thing" there was a price to pay. The store was a huge souvenir shop, with thousands of square feet of trinkets and oddities to take home as gifts. The front counter was staffed by two cashiers, and their registers were busily collecting the money necessary to make the lease payments on those sixty miles of billboards.

As I rummaged through the sea-shell clocks, leather bull-whips, and onyx chess sets for a gift to take home to my wife, I caught a glimpse of my friend John disappearing through the gate. I wasn't surprised; he was always the adventurous type. When my other friend Kim, realized what John had done, he didn't want to be left out and tried to talk me into doing it. If I would, he would. You know, the safety-in-numbers kind of a thing.

He finally convinced me that we were old enough to waste our money if we wanted to, and after all, we had come a long way. We were so close now it didn't seem to make much difference anyway. We would be able to tell all of our friends about it. When we were discussing the price, the cashier leaned over and whispered, "It's almost free." To my surprise, at that point, the decision seemed easy and we went in.

Once a young man and woman went in to see their bishop. They were practically walking on air. Their eyes sparkled brightly, and they each had those permanent grins that make your cheeks hurt just to look at. They proceeded to tell the bishop about their plans to be married. The bishop was happy for them. It was obvious they were deeply in love. They talked of their desire to have a marriage Heavenly Father would approve of and that they had been prayed together seeking inspiration about that important decision. They said they were studying the scriptures together regularly and that they were sure their union was made in heaven. It's a beautiful sight to see two people so much in love, and the bishop felt the Holy Ghost present as they discussed the importance of the marriage covenant. The young couple held hands throughout the interview and looked dreamily into each other's eyes.

Marriage is a sacred institution. When blessed by our Father in Heaven, it can be an eternal partnership of joy and happiness within the new and everlasting covenant of marriage. *"Therefore shall a man leave his father and his mother, and shall cleave unto his wife: and they shall be one flesh." (Genesis 2:24)* We are also commanded to *"..Be fruitful, and multiply, and replenish the earth..." (Genesis 1:28)*

In the pamphlet, For The Strength of Youth, we have been counseled that sexual intimacy should be reserved for Heavenly Father's children within the bonds of marriage. The physical relationship between a husband and wife can be beautiful and sacred. It is ordained of God for the procreation of children and for the expression of love within a marriage. Because sexual intimacy is so sacred, the Lord requires self-control and purity before marriage as well as full fidelity after marriage. In dating we are taught to treat our date with respect, and have the same respect shown in return. Never treat your date as an object to be used for your own lustful desires or ego. Improper physical contact can cause a loss of self control. Always stay in control of yourself and your feelings.

The bishop felt inspired to counsel the couple about spending too much time alone before their wedding. He gave them a list of 'Celestial Dating Rules,' and asked them to commit to following them. He explained the danger of tempting their obvious passion. For *"...whatsoever thing persuadeth men to do evil,... ye may know with a perfect knowledge it is of the devil..." (Moroni 7:17)*

In the world today, the sexual relationship between a man and a woman, is distorted, degraded, and abused to an unprecedented degree. It has become the basic story line for comics and writers alike, and is portrayed in movies and on television every day as permissible at anytime, anyplace, and with anyone.

About a week after the bishop had his interview with the love-struck couple, he received an urgent phone call late at night. There had been an incident. The bishop rushed down to the church, and there, in the same office, on the same chairs, sat the same two children of our Heavenly Father. Their sparkly eyes were now red and puffy, and their bubbly personalities had given way to grief and despair. Their heads hung low, and tears blurred their once clear gaze. Sorrow had replaced their happiness because they allowed temptation to influence their decisions.

The choice to live the law of chastity is ours. Our bishops can't make that decision for us. Our parents and friends can't either. And Satan has no control over us, unless we give it to him.

As we travel along that straight and narrow highway that leads to eternal life, stay true to the faith. At times the road to a celestial marriage seems long and never ending. And all the while Satan is doing a sinister job of advertising and recruiting followers. But know this, his only goal is to make us miserable. There is no doubt, some of his billboards are clever, attractive, and humorous. You may have started your journey with a strong testimony and a determination to resist temptation, but if you allow him to occupy more and more of your thoughts, and allow wickedness to become the popular topic of your conversations, you may find yourself following the crowd off the wrong exit. You may be hanging around so close to temptation, browsing with curiosity, that by the time you consider the price of sin, it almost seems free.

To this day I am embarrassed about falling for the marketing scam of "The Thing." My wife read this story and asked what The Thing was, and the ironic part of the whole story is, I can't remember. I guess that fact alone should confirm that it wasn't worth the price I paid.

The price for committing sexual transgressions is high. If you will follow the Savior and the promptings of the Holy Ghost at every turn in life, avoiding the sorrow of sin will be no big *thing*.

Fooseball From Heaven

It's not unusual for someone to come up after I give a talk and ask, "Was that a true story?"

Janice and I were about a week away from our wedding date and we were driving around in Denver. In conversation I mentioned something about my past, and she was shocked. I pulled the car over and told her this, 'We will be sitting on the porch, with our teeth in a glass, and I'll tell you one you haven't heard before.'

When I die, don't grieve over this guy, I've lived a full life, again and again and again.

"...things which they had beheld with an eye of faith, and they were glad." (Ether 12:19)

On June twenty-eighth, 1975, at 1:20 in the morning, there was an accident. I was living in LaJolla, California at the time and my mother called me on the phone, "Are you sitting down?" Those aren't the words you want to hear first in a conversation. "No," I said, "What's the matter?" She proceeded to tell me about what happened in the Glenwood Canyon, just a few miles East of Glenwood Springs, Colorado. Back then, Interstate 70 wasn't the super-structure of tunnels and double-decker freeway that it is today. It was a two-lane highway that took the lives of many people.

A jeep carrying four very close friends of mine had rolled over repeatedly, leaving its passengers strewn along the road in various degrees of devastation. Debbie was the first to regain consciousness. Her knee was severely damaged and one of her ears was practically torn from the side of her head. Bleeding, and in shock, she managed to find Ricky Lee and pull him off of the road. Rick's most noticeable injury was a severe head laceration. The other two passengers Mike and Scott didn't survive.

When my mother told me the details of the accident, I was more than a thousand miles away, but I could feel the concern she had for me. She wanted to make sure I wasn't alone. She was worried how I would react. I was sorry Debbie and Rick were hurt, but it sounded like they were going to be all right. The loss of Mike and Scott was devastating.

Scott was one of my best friends. I dated his sister in high school and became a close friend of his family. Scott and I spent a lot of fun times together, hiking, spelunking, four-wheeling, rock climbing and having other adventures. But the binding relationship we shared was in the steep and deep of the Rocky Mountains, skiing powder.

Skiing is the sport of choice in the heart of the Rockies. And though you could find Scott and me skiing at the local areas, providing entertainment for the other skiers that were riding up the lifts, more often than not, we were hidden from the public eye. We had a habit of getting away, leaving the groomed trails that provided a safe environment, and slipping into the trees, out of bounds. We spent most of our time there. We even climbed undeveloped mountains just to experience the thrill of extreme skiing. We were hungry for untouched powder and the serenity of the frozen wonderland. That was where Scott and I grew so close.

I'm not advocating the sport of extreme skiing or telling anyone that it's okay to ski out of bounds. Many states and ski areas will prosecute you for such a thing, while it is acceptable in others. In any event, it's a dangerous sport. That's why Scott and I made such a good team.

If someone goes skiing alone out of bounds, a simple fall, or loosing a ski, could cost them their life. When the snow is deep it's impossible to walk through and the snow covering the trees can muffle even the loudest scream for help. A person could easily die of hypothermia before anyone finds them. Scott and I had a pact. We promised one another that neither of us would ever leave the other alone on a mountain.

I was born in Aspen, Colorado, and from what I remember, I was born with skis on (sorry Mom.) It wasn't always easy for me to find someone I enjoyed skiing with. I needed someone who could keep up, a person who was comfortable in the trees. Scott was like my shadow. Our skiing styles were incredibly similar. Turn for turn, we stayed together. We almost anticipated which side of a tree the other would turn around. If Scott went right, I went left, and we met on the other side. I could almost pick out where he would jump a cornice. We knew our sport was dangerous and we took it seriously. We watched out for each other. And now he was gone. He left me behind. My partner was dead, and at such a young age.

I flew back to Colorado for the services. The night before Scott's funeral, his family arranged for a viewing. It was one last chance for his friends and family to see him. I went to pay my respects and try to console his family in their grief, but what could I say? When I looked into his casket, his neatly folded hands were holding a small piece of sagebrush. I found out his sister put it in there as a token of love for her brother.

When Scott's family was going to take a vacation, he would venture up the mountain behind his house and pick some sagebrush to hang in their car. He loved the smell of it. I thought it was pretty cool of his sister to think of it. When I got home from the viewing, I couldn't stop thinking about it. What a great idea. It reminded me of some cultures that bury their dead with provisions for the long journey home.

I paced in my room looking for something I could put inside his casket. I wanted to show the love I had for him. My skies were too long or I would have put them in. I looked at the fooseball table that was still sitting in my old room. Many nights, Scott and I stood at that table, beating any number of challengers. We loved to play that game, and though it wasn't a ski which would have better represented our relationship, it was definitely a token of my love for my friend. I grabbed a ball from the table and ran back to the funeral home. I asked his parents for permission, and carefully placed the fooseball into his casket. I told him it was a symbol of our friendship, and that I would always remember him. The whole situation made me wonder where he was going. Would I ever see him again? Was this the end of my friend? It seemed like a waste. He had such potential.

A few months later I was having a difficult time in my life. I was living in Mammoth Lakes, California. I was drifting further and further from the trail the Savior had groomed for me. I was slipping off the path of safety and out-of-bounds. I was forgetting the testimony of my youth. I still believed in God and knew that Jesus Christ was my Savior, but that belief was tucked away. I didn't ever think about it. I didn't let those kinds of things influence the choices I was making. I didn't think much about a life after death, I was focused on the 'now.' I was only interested in personal gratification. My happiness depended on me, and it was a full time job taking care of that. And my idea of heaven was either steep, submergible powder, or a ski run that had such big moguls it looked like a stack of vertical Volkswagens. In relation to the true meaning of life, I was lost.

One day I turned to what I considered my religion, I went skiing. I needed to find some peace in my troubled world. Once again, the crisp air of the mountain and the physical demand of skiing took away my stress. I was about half way down the mountain and had just finished skiing a great trail. If anyone had asked me, I would have told them that life couldn't get any better. I don't know why I looked down, but there in the snow was the most incredible thing I have ever seen. It was a fooseball.

I wasn't a member of any church. I wasn't in the habit of praying or reading scriptures or anything like unto it. But when I bent over and picked up that little ball, I believed. I wasn't sure what I believed, but I believed.

I didn't think that it fell from heaven, or that Scott had mysteriously placed it there. I figured some other skier must have stolen it from a fooseball table in a bar the night before. I figured that when that fooseball thief woke up in the morning, he shook off his hang-over and just happened to come up skiing. And for some unknown reason, that same guy just happened to drop the fooseball, strategically, so that it wouldn't get covered up by the billion tons of snow all around it, and that when I just happened to stop in the same spot, and just HAPPENED to look down, I would find it.

I can't tell you that I turned my life around because of that experience, but as it often happens with the death of a loved one, or finding round things on a mountain, I started thinking about heaven and the things I was taught while I was growing up. There was more to life than a good day of skiing, and there was more to life-after-death, than I was considering during that period of my life.

Scott was my friend and I miss him. His family planted a tiny little tree by his grave all those years ago. I haven't seen it lately but I'll bet it's huge by now. I know I will see my friend again, and when I do, I'll have an opportunity to thank him for keeping his promise. He came back for me, when I fell.

A Testimony Of Flowers

This poem was written for Mike Holdaway.
May the memory of one very special, Master Gardener, live on.

"Yea, and the herb, and the good things which come of the earth,
whether for food or for rainment, or for houses, or for barns,
or for orchards, or for gardens, or for vineyards;
Yea, all things which come of the earth, in the season thereof,
are made for the benefit and the use of man,
both to please the eye and to gladden the heart;"
(D&C 59:17-18)

A Testimony Of Flowers

I've often seen flowers turn sadness to joy,
like the effect of a puppy on a girl or a boy.
We pick them for lovers, for friends who are in need,
and that miracle, that magic, began with a seed.
It was all made possible by the faith of one,
who planted the seed, who had a green thumb.
He nurtured and cared for each tender sprout,
until their real beauty came blossoming out.
And what makes the gardener so happy each day?
To make arrangements of love, and then give them away.

I'm Okay

I always say, 'I may not be good, but I'm slow.'
For some reason I tend to learn things the hard way.
I'm one of those dads that reads the directions to the swing-set,
after I build it my way.

"If ye love me, keep my commandments."
(John 14:15)

It was a beautiful Summit County day in Colorado. The sky was blue and the fall colors were just starting to change. I was driving around the Dillon Reservoir from Breckenridge to the little town of Frisco. There was very little traffic on Highway 9 that day, but in front of me was a pick-up truck with a camper on the back. We were both traveling at about fifty-five miles per hour. Suddenly, to my horror the back door on the camper opened up and a man stepped out. I will never forget watching him tumble down the highway like a rag doll. It was all I could do to swerve and avoid running over him.

I slammed on my brakes, and by the time I stopped and jumped out of my truck, the man was on his feet staggering around in circles. He looked like he didn't know which way was up, and he was bleeding from a cut on his head. I grabbed him by the arm and told him to lie down. "No, no, I'm okay," the words spun from his mouth. But I knew he wasn't. One of his hands was obviously broken. "Sir, you're hurt. You need to lie down,' I urged. But once again his reply was, "No, I'm okay. I just need to rest. I'll be fine."

Soon, another car stopped and together the driver and I convinced the injured man to get into my truck. Since it was only a couple of miles to the Summit Medical Center, I felt it was quicker to drive him myself rather than send for an ambulance. During the ride the man did his best to convince me he was all right. He said none of his injuries were serious. "It's just a scratch," he said. Once inside the emergency room, the doctors wanted to take x-rays, but he resisted. Without the man's consent, they were unable to help him.

The last time I saw him he was alone, and limping down the narrow mountain highway near the hospital. Without the doctors having the opportunity to evaluate his injuries, it was impossible to know just how serious they were. He could have had some internal injuries and without the proper care, they could be fatal. I often wonder what became of him.

There was no doubt in my mind that the man was intoxicated. I think I got a buzz just from the smell of alcohol that followed him into my truck. He told me that he and some friends were staying at a campground on the Blue River. That was all he could remember. Here is the story as I see it. After he and his buddies did a little too much partying, this guy decided to go into the camper and sleep it off (or pass out.) While he was snoozing in the back, his friends must have decided to make a run into town. Well, when he woke up, he must have had an urgent need to 'visit Mother Nature,' and that was when Snoozey opened the door and stepped out. For me, that move brings a whole new meaning to the phrase, 'Watch out for that first step.' It was a dooooooozy!

That experience reminded me how many of us share similar traits with the man who stepped out of the camper. Some of us are injured, confused or spiritually disoriented. We may be hurting, yet refuse to accept the help of anyone. We may resist the counsel from our priesthood leaders, even the words of the Prophet. Our happiness and salvation may be in serious danger, but because of our intense desire to be independent, we reject Christ's plea when He said, *"If ye love me, keep my commandments." (John 14:15).* When we fail to keep the commandments, we stumble around in circles like we are lost. And when we are asked how we are doing, we say it over and over, "I'm okay, I'll be all right." We choose to ignore the spiritual injuries and the breaking of our testimonies.

Why would anyone be so careless? What would motivate someone to take that first step? Once in a while, it is the first step that sends us tumbling down a dangerous road. When we fall, how can we be so stubborn that we refuse the helping hand of a loved one? Why do we try so hard to solve our problems on our own? Why are we unwilling to surrender them to the Lord and accept His offer. *"Trust in the Lord with all thine heart; and lean not unto thine own understanding. In all thy ways acknowledge him, and he shall direct thy paths." (Proverbs 3:5-6)*

When we accept that we are in need of spiritual help, the quickest first-aid is prayer. Heavenly Father is always there for us and prayer is one way to show our humility and our dependence on Him.

A good place to find a spiritual doctor or nurse is our ward family. I am constantly amazed at the acts of kindness and generosity that I see demonstrated every week by members of the Church.

Our bishops are like specialists or surgeons. They take care of all of our serious injuries. They have the authority and responsibility to administer over their wards and to care for the sick and the down-trodden.

The Prophet and those that serve with him administer the affairs of this Life-giving gospel. General conference is held every six months for members of the Church and non-members around the world to listen to the servants of the Lord. We have a chance to sit at the feet of a living Prophet and to be taught the ways of truth and righteousness. I can't imagine my life without it.

I had a friend of mine invite me to accompany him to general conference shortly after I joined the Church. It was only an eight hour drive from my home in Colorado. We were standing in the center of the Tabernacle, in Salt Lake City, waiting for the session to begin. Everyone was visiting with the people around them who were from many different parts of the world. Spencer W. Kimball was the president of the Church at the time and his health was such that he hadn't attended a session of conference for quite some time. People were so used to hearing that he was watching the proceedings from the Hotel Utah, that they didn't expect him to be there. Because the acoustics in the Tabernacle are so amazing, the socializing of the congregation was really getting loud. The door to the left of the pulpit opened and two men walked through the door helping a third man. The room went from a dull roar, to total silence in an instant. You could have heard a butterfly in flight had there been one in the room. I will never forget the feeling the first time I was in the presence of a living Prophet. On the way home from Salt Lake City, I remember telling my friend, "If I ever have the chance to attend conference again, I'll walk to Salt Lake if I have to." I've never had to walk, but I have spent more than 450 hours standing in line or sitting on those hard benches in the Tabernacle just to absorb the feeling of being near the Prophet. I have loved every minute of it.

Not all of God's children believe it is possible to have a living Prophet today. Not everyone believes we need one. To some, even mentioning the word 'prophet' sends them into a panic. But Heavenly Father loves us as much today as he did in the days of the ancient prophets. Not many people will argue that considering the influence of wickedness in the world today, we need a prophet as much or more that they did in the time of Noah. Someone to call us to repentance, and to lead us in the ways of righteousness. It is unfortunate that not all members of the Church take general conference as seriously as they should.

In the Book of Mormon, one of my favorite stories is that of King Benjamin. Before he died he wanted his son Mosiah to call the people of Zarahemla together, and to give them a farewell address. That story reminds me of general conference.

The King sent a proclamation throughout the land, so that everyone knew the time and the place.

Today conference is always held the first weekend in April and October.

The people of Zarahemla had multiplied exceedingly and had waxed great in the land.

The Church today has increased exceedingly, and there are an enormous numbers of converts every year.

King Benjamin called them to the temple, *"...every man according to his family, consisting of his wife, and his sons, and his daughters..., from the eldest down to the youngest..."*

General conference is also for the whole family.

"And they pitched their tents round about the temple, every man having his tent with the door thereof toward the temple, that thereby they might remain in their tents and hear the words..."

We should pay attention to the messages of conference.

And *"the multitude being so great that king Benjamin could not teach them all within the walls of the temple..."* so he built a tower.

The Church uses satellites and televisions, *"...thereby his people might hear the words which he should speak unto them."*

"They could not all hear his words because of the greatness of the multitude; therefore he caused that the words which he spake should be written and sent forth among those that were not under the sound of his voice, that they might also receive his words."

Today, the words of conference are sent forth in the Ensign magazine.

Then King Benjamin taught, *"...I have not commanded you to come up hither to trifle with the words which I shall speak, but that you should harken unto me, and open your ears that ye may hear, and your hearts that ye may understand, and your minds that the mysteries of God may be unfolded to your view."* What a powerful statement. After that, he proceeded to teach the principles of the gospel, starting with service. *"...when ye are in the service of your fellow beings ye are only in the service of your God." (Mosiah 2:17)*

There were probably some who received the proclamation from King Benjamin about the upcoming conference, but went out hunting anyway. Sometimes I hear people talk as if it's a vacation day, a day off from church.

Nevertheless, I'm sure some things back then were a lot like they are now. I for one, would love to have been there to hear the words of King Benjamin echoing throughout the walls of the temple.

"I say unto you, my brethren, that if you should render all the thanks and praise which your whole soul has power to possess, to that God who has created you, and has kept and preserved you, and has caused that ye should rejoice, and

has granted that ye should live in peace one with another...I say unto you that if ye should serve him who has created you from the beginning, and is preserving you from day to day, by lending you breath, that ye may live and move and do according to your own will, and even supporting you from one moment to another...I say, if ye should serve him with all your whole souls yet ye would be unprofitable servants. And behold, all that he requires of you is to keep his commandments; and he has promised you that if ye would keep his commandments ye should prosper in the land; and he never doth vary from that which he hath said; therefore, if ye do keep his commandments he doth bless you and prosper you." (Mosiah 2:20-22)

I can hear King Benjamin giving that talk in the Tabernacle. His counsel is as good today as it was then.

"And moreover, I would desire that ye should consider on the blessed and happy state of those that keep the commandments of God. For behold, they are blessed in all things, both temporal and spiritual; and if they hold out faithful to the end they are received into heaven, that thereby they may dwell with God in a state of never-ending happiness. O remember, remember that these things are true; for the Lord God hath spoken it." (Mosiah 2:41)

Life is too short to live in pain. The Lord has prepared to take care of our every need and to wipe away our tears. If you are limping down a lonely highway in this life, turn around and treat yourself to some intensive care. Let the Good Doctor mend your broken spirit, dress your wounds, and apply the Balm of Gilead. Don't ignore any loss of the Holy Spirit from your countenance.

"For the natural man is an enemy to God, and has been from the fall of Adam, and will be, forever and ever, unless he yields to the enticings of the Holy Spirit, and putteth off the natural man and becometh a saint through the atonement of Christ the Lord, and becometh as a child, submissive, meek, humble, patient, full of love, willing to submit to all things which the Lord seeth fit to inflict upon him, even as a child doth submit to his father." (Mosiah 3:19)

" and men are, that they might have joy!" (2 Nephi 2:25)

"Counsel with the Lord in all thy doings, and he will direct thee for good;
yea, when thou liest down at night, (even in a camper) *lie down unto the Lord,*
that he may watch over you in your sleep; and when thou risest in the morning
let thy heart be full of thanks unto God; and if ye do these things,
ye shall be lifted up at the last day."
(Alma 37:37)

By Its Cover

*This is the only story in Cheap Sunglasses that I made up.
I added it because it has been so popular.
Rather than chance the possibility of offending anyone,
I used myself as the one who judged others.*

*"Judge not, that ye be not judged."
(Matthew 7:1)*

The scriptures are filled with lessons on the topic of judging others and we would be wise to heed the words of the Lord, as spoken by the prophets; *"Love one another," "Serve one another,"* and *"Be not a respector of persons."* For we are all children of the same God, equal to the angels, and can become heirs to all that our Father hath, if we learn to be more like him.

Situation #1: I got up really early the other day to go water skiing, but having pushed the snooze button one-too-many times, I was late to meet my friends. I was taking advantage of the empty streets in my little S10 pick-up, trying to make up all the time I could. I was shocked when I rounded a corner and saw some teenagers still out walking the streets. They looked as though they hadn't been home all night and were either very tired or under the influence of drugs. What could they possibly have been up to all night; out partying, vandalizing, or just plain 'no good.' I can't believe some parents; why they ever had children in the first place is beyond me. I think if they're going to allow their children to wander the streets all night, the children should be taken and given to someone who will raise them with some values.

Another Perspective: Our stake has a wonderful seminary program, staffed by gifted teachers who genuinely care about our youth and their futures. Our senior class has a tradition of getting together at Sister Rosenlof's house for an all night, scripture read-a-thon. Last night the students made an attempt to read The Book of Mormon, cover-to-cover in one night. These students are wonderful young men and women who hunger for opportunities to strengthen their testimonies and develop a better understanding of the gospel. After reading all night, they finally called it quits. Two of the young men offered to walk some of the young women home. After all, it was still very early in the morning and it might not have been safe for the girls to walk home alone. As they were walking down the street, a white S10 pick-up went flying by, and one of the young men said, "I guess we better stay on the sidewalk. It looks like some of the drunks are still out!"

Situation #2: My wife and I were driving home from 'date night,' late last Friday in our big black Suburban. We noticed a man who looked like he was in a hurry walking through our neighborhood. He had a brown paper bag in his hand, you know the kind I'm talking about, twisted around the top of what appeared to be a bottle. (Booze, I'm sure.) "He looks like he can't wait to get home and drown his sorrows," I said in an acerbic tone. My wife hit the power door locks and snapped, "Don't slow down!" I didn't recognize the stranger and I have always hated to see that kind of element so close to home. We live in a respectable neighborhood, and we want to keep it the kind of place fit to raise a family. Ever since they built those apartments down the street, these kinds of losers wander through here more often. I said, "We'd better get our alarm fixed; he's probably a thief looking for an easy target."

Another Perspective: It was late and Rich was walking as fast as he could. The only thing on his mind was the phone call he just received and the urgency in the young father's voice. He had practically begged Rich to come over to his house. There was nothing unusual about his request, but Rich was new in town and the two men had just met the week before. It never occurred to Rich to mention that when he answered the phone, he was sitting at the kitchen table rebuilding the carburetor for his only car. And even if he walked, he would have to make one stop on the way. His answer was a confident, "I'll be right there." With faith and determination he started walking in the direction of the young man's apartment. Along the way there was a twenty-four hour grocery store, and it wasn't long before Rich was hustling out of the automatic doors carrying a brown paper bag which he nervously twisted in his hands. He might have been concerned about the lateness of the hour, but he was in a nice neighborhood, with nice people, and he was on an errand for the Lord. The words "Please hurry," played over and over in his mind as he tried to prepare for and contemplate his worthiness to perform a priesthood ordinance. He also made a quiet commitment to himself, to never again be caught without some consecrated oil in the house. Just about that time, a big black Suburban rushed by without slowing down.

Situation #3: It was almost dark when I sat down beneath a tree to rest my weary legs. I had only a small stream to cross, and soon I would be back within the city limits. I had spent most of the afternoon hiking around on the mountain. I needed some time alone, and have always considered hiking a productive way to keep myself physically and mentally fit. After a few minutes, I heard a sound coming from the slope below me. I noticed four men winding their way up the mountain. They were still quite a distance away and I was sure they hadn't seen me silhouetted against the olive tree. Though my view of the city was magnificent, and the first stars of the evening were flickering overhead, I couldn't keep my attention from the ascending group. It was not unusual to have people who have no other place to stay wander out of town at sundown looking for a safe place to sleep for the night. As they got closer I could see that they were not in any hurry. Slowly placing one foot in front of the other, they appeared to have no where else to go. They looked as if they hadn't a care in the world. What a life I thought, no stress and no worries. Don't get me wrong. It's not that I'm cold-blooded; I have compassion for the homeless. It breaks my heart to think that some people have very little chance to become successful at anything. And they will probably never have an opportunity to do anything in this life worth mentioning. Then as I suspected, three of them looked as though they were settling down for a good night's sleep.The fourth one continued in my direction. Barefoot and bedraggled, with both long hair and a beard, this one looked like he had drunk one too many glasses of wine. He walked as though his legs were about to buckle, almost like he was carrying the weight of the world on his shoulders. Suddenly he collapsed to his knees, and buried his head in his hands. It gets to me every time I see a guy like that, wasting his life. He looked like he was in his thirties, and in good enough health to go out and get a job. You know what I mean, pull his own weight. Why can't everyone live up to the measure of their creation?

Another Perspective: Tradition still identifies a garden some two hundred and fifty yards east of the city wall. And *"...he went forth with his disciples over the brook Cedron, where was a garden, into the which he entered, and his disciples." (John 18:1) And there on the slope of The Mount of Olives, lies Gethsemane. "And he was withdrawn from them about a stone's cast..." (Luke 22:41) "...[he] fell on the ground, and prayed..." (Mark 14:35)* It was there that Jesus Christ, the son of the living God knelt in prayer. And while his disciples slept, he suffered as no man can even imagine. In agony, and bleeding from every pore, he took upon himself the sins of the world. In one humble, selfless act of love, the salvation of every person who ever lived upon the face of the Earth, or ever will live upon the Earth, was made possible.

All of God's children were created equally. We are each unique individuals. As we tarry through this marvelous second estate, let us look upon each of our Father's children with kindness and respect. We may feel that we are experts at first impressions, and that no one can equal our judge of character, but until we have walked a mile in another man's shoes, until we have lived his life, we really have no idea who he is, or why he is that way. How thankful I am to know that Jesus Christ will be my judge, *"For the Father judgeth no man, but hath committed all judgment unto the Son." (John 5:22) And he will be compassionate and merciful. And "...the judgments of him that is just shall rest upon them." (2 Nephi 1:10)* I know that first and foremost, before ever casting his judgment upon me, that He will love me. He has always loved me. Love one another.

The Primary song, *"I'm Trying To Be Like Jesus"*, expresses this idea perfectly.

I'm trying to be like Jesus; I'm following in His ways.
I'm trying to love as He did, in all that I do and say.
At times I am tempted to make a wrong choice,
But I try to listen as the still small voice whispers,
Love one another as Jesus loves you.
Try to show kindness in all that you do.
Be gentle and loving in deed and in thought,
For these are the things Jesus taught.
I'm trying to love my neighbor;
I'm learning to serve my friends.
I watch for the day of gladness,
When Jesus will come again.
I try to remember the lessons He taught,
Then the Holy Spirit enters into my thoughts, saying;
Love one another as Jesus loves you.
Try to show kindness in all that you do.
Be gentle and loving in deed and in thought,
For these are the things we are taught.

'I'm Trying To Be Like Jesus', Words and Music: Janice Kapp Perry, b. 1938.

All That Is Love

This poem was written for Richard Paul Evans
who encourages me to write with 'paper and pencil'.
He said, "There's something organic about it."

All That Is Love

As the still small voice of the Spirit,
sweeps us from day to day;
And the simple joys of everyday life,
wrap us deeper in the arms of the Savior;
Watch for the angels of promise,
that declare gifts from above;
And follow...humbly...all that is bright and true,
all that is love.

Wrong Side Of The Fence

When I served as a bishop the greatest lesson I learned was that of forgiveness.
If I don't learn to forgive, how can I expect to be forgiven?
Anyone can stray from the comfort of the Gospel,
and anyone can come back.
The hard part for some of us, is signing up for the
Welcoming Committee.

"...wickedness never was happiness."
(Alma 41:10)

One day in my youth, I was working as a painter in Aspen Colorado. The Roaring Fork Valley is a beautiful place, surrounded by mountains covered with evergreen and aspen trees. I walked outside to get some supplies from our paint-van, when I noticed something strange happening across the street. There was a deer pacing back and forth behind a chain link fence. Though seeing a deer in Colorado wasn't anything new, this deer's curiosity had taken him into town and into a dangerous situation. It had left the security of the forest and was stuck in a life threatening situation. The deer was in the storage yard of a large utility company. There, among the huge spools of wire and parked trucks, the deer was out of its element. The equipment must have been valuable because the company had gone to great expense to build a tall chain link fence all the way around the yard. For added protection there were strands of barbed wire on the top of the fence, angled to the inside of the yard. It was a regular fortress considering the area had very little crime.

Whatever the reason or circumstances that led to the deer being stuck behind the fence didn't seem as important as how it was going to get out. It looked nervous as it paced back and forth, never taking its eyes off the hillside beyond the fence. That was home and safety. That was where it belonged, on the other side of the fence. The deer longed for freedom and knew it was in a bad place, but it had no idea how to get out. The comfort and safety of the forest was right there in front of it, but getting there seemed to be an impossible task. It may or may not have missed the herd, but there was no doubt that it wanted out of town.

All at once the deer sprung from the ground in an effort to jump the fence. It didn't even get close. It fell back into the yard, landing on its back with a thud. I noticed some men in the yard watching the deer struggle to its feet. They were whistling, clapping their hands, and trying to herd the deer toward an open gate on the side of the yard. The double-wide gate was built big enough to allow the company's trucks and delivery vehicles access to the yard. It was a perfect escape route for the deer. From the open gate there was nothing else to stop it from running back to the forest. But even with the encouragement of those who were trying to help, the deer continued with its quest. It saw one and only one way to get out, and that was uphill. A few times the men in the yard managed to get the deer away from the fence, but in a panic, it almost trampled the same men who were trying to save its life as it lunged back at the fence. The natural instincts of the deer were too strong. It could see the trees through the fence, but was unable to see the danger in its path. The easiest and safest way out, was obvious to everyone, except the deer.

With a burst of speed the deer made another attempt to jump the fence. Once again it came crashing to the ground in disarray, legs and hoofs pointing in every direction. Quickly, without taking time to recover, it jumped again but didn't have the strength to clear the fence. For a moment the deer got hung up in the barbed wire but managed to shake free, only to land with its head bent the wrong way.

Curiosity and concern led me across the street to help. The closer I got, the more I realized I didn't have any great ideas. The gate was already wide open, it was broad daylight and there were plenty of people trying to help. I suggested to the men that the more they tried scaring the deer out of the yard, the more disoriented it was getting. I thought they should try backing off a little, and let the deer calm down. All of us wanted the deer to stop making its futile attempts at the fence. Maybe later, on its own it would walk by the gate and get out safely. Unfortunately, there was also the possibility that the deer might stay on the wrong side of the fence. Without nourishment, it would die.

Even when the men stopped clapping and shouting, the deer continued to charge the fence. Again and again it jumped, and over and over it crashed to the ground. I was close enough now to see the misery in its eyes. It was getting weaker and was visibly distressed. From my new vantage point I could see that its mouth was torn and bleeding. With every leap for freedom, using every ounce of its strength, the deer was jumping just high enough to catch the top strand of barbed wire in its mouth. The sharp points on the wire tore the corners of the deer's mouth and with each jump, they ripped deeper.

Why did it continue to jump? It was only getting hurt. It was slowly killing itself, jumping, getting cut, falling, and crashing. Why didn't it look for a better way? Why didn't it just turn away from the fence and walk out?

Finally, with what must have been a do-or-die leap, the deer managed to get its front legs up and over the top strand of barbed-wire. It hung there, frantically twisting and turning itself into a knot. It wasn't anything at all like the grace and ease you have seen on television when deer jump fences in slow motion, clearing them by a mile.
When the deer shook loose from the barbed-wire it dropped to the ground. I was almost happy to see it land face first in the dirt. At least it

was free from the deadly clutches of the barbed wire. And better than that, to my surprise it had managed to twist and roll over the fence. It was outside the fence. It was free. Staggering to its feet, it headed up the hill into the forest without looking back.

What happened to the deer after that is left up to your imagination. You may believe that the deer walked a short distance into the forest and curled up in the shade of an aspen grove. Maybe it licked its wounds, rested, and eventually recovered completely. You may imagine the deer deep in the forest, in a safe place, enjoying a long life of freedom. You may see the deer as stronger and wiser from its experience, and able to use that experience for the benefit of the herd; a stronger, wiser, and more understanding leader. It all sounds so beneficial, so worthwhile. Even the scars in the corner of the deer's mouth, seem to fade with time. You may say it wasn't so bad on the other side of the fence... just for a little while.

But not everyone imagines this story ending the same way. What if the deer had sustained deep internal injuries during its many crash landings. What if the cuts in its mouth became infected, and never healed. It could have easily broken some bones, which would cause it to fall prey to a predator such as a mountain lion.

Not everyone lets their curiosity take them to the wrong side of the fence. But there are those of us who have wandered out of the safety of the woods. Though our experiences are different, when we find ourselves on the wrong side, we know we are there. Unfortunately, even after we realize it and we'd do anything to get back, it may be easier to say than to do.

When we cross the fence of morality, or break the Word of Wisdom, even once with the attitude that we will have a little fun, then repent, we are making a terrible mistake. When we are stuck in an environment that lacks spiritual nourishment, we become weaker, and weaker, and if we remain there, we will eventually die a spiritual death. The obstacles that stand between us and happiness start looking like barbed wire fences, designed by Satan to keep us in a yard of suffering. If you have found yourself on the wrong side of the fence, and if every time you make an effort to escape, you get knocked back down, look around to those who are trying to help you. Look to those who can guide you through the open gate to the freedom and safety you are longing for. It doesn't have to cost you your life. The Savior has already paid the price with His life.

If the deer hadn't had a deep desire to go home, it would have stayed in the yard. If we stay on the wrong side long enough we could lose the desire to go home and end up venturing farther into town.

Some people I've met in the last seventeen years, find it hard to believe I had such a terrible visit on the other side of the fence. The gospel has a wonderful way of healing scars. The Savior is so forgiving. I'm so lucky. As the Savior so beautifully puts it, *"Come unto me, all [ye] that labour and are heavy laden, and I will give you rest." (Matthew 11:28)*

I will always be thankful for the miracle of forgiveness, and for the compassion of a loving Heavenly Father. I know if it weren't for the gospel of Jesus Christ, I would have died with nothing more than a distant view of happiness through a chain link fence.

In the cool shade, beneath the trees of knowledge, near the spring of love that never faileth, together with an eternal family of does, bucks, and fawns, you can inherit all that Heavenly Father has for you. He has provided for your every need. There is no obstacle placed before you, no matter where you have wandered, that you can not conquer.

The Windmill

At different times in your life
you may have felt like one of the early settlers of the Netherlands,
clinging to the very ground on which you stand.
You may have spent years building a foundation on which to raise a family,
cultivating fields of understanding, and fighting the tides of adversity.
When the winds of change beat against you,
and the tides of destruction try to take it all away,
it is faith, hope and love that will help you stand your ground.

"And faith, hope, charity and love, with an eye single to the glory of God
qualify him for the work."
(D&C 4:5)

The Windmill

As the winds of change beat relentlessly against my quiet and content spirit,
my very frame shakes and shudders at the gale.
I stand on the shoreline of troubled waters,
and often harbor feelings of hopelessness,
as one without cause or reason.
But as I stretch forth my blades,
blades of faith, and hope, and love,
I harness all that life has blown in my direction,
and create within,
the strength to grow, the power to move on,
and the industry to succeed.
It matters not if I pump the endless waters of tribulation,
or fight an intruding sea of destruction.
I don't care if I merely grind the grains of reality,
or simply expand the resources of another.
Just the simple fact that I exist,
that I can turn, or move at all,
creates the warm feeling of possibility,
the possibility of growth, of life, of happiness.
So let the winds blow, let the times change,
go ahead, make me stronger, more productive.
I will spin faster because I am free,
I will work harder against the greater force.
I will stand firm and never run.
I have a place and a purpose.
The next time you feel you're losing ground,
or that your emotional foundation is in danger,
when the trials of life close in on you,
and challenge your happiness,
Remember the windmill.
Stand tall,
hold your ground,
and turn with the inevitable change of the winds.
Spin a testimony of possibilities.

The Burning Within

The third week of July every summer, the town of New Castle, Colorado celebrates Burning Mountain Days. On the eighth of June every year I celebrate my baptism.

"...Did not our hearts burn within us, while he talked with us by the way, and while he opened to us the scriptures?"
(Luke 24:32)

There was an explosion in the Vulcan Mine on February 18, 1896. A miner by the name of Ed Welch was nearly a quarter of a mile inside that dirty coal mine when the explosion blew him all the way out, out of that dangerous pit of darkness and into the light. Many others were not so fortunate. Some died. Later there was an attempt to mine another section of the vein, but a second explosion closed the Vulcan forever. A fire which started as a result of that explosion is still burning today over a hundred years later. Many have tried to put the fire out, but to this day, it burns hotter than ever. Mine experts are of the opinion that it is a fire that will never burn out. Ward's Peak, the mountain in which the fire burns is now called, "The Burning Mountain." It will never be the same. I went to high school just up the Colorado River from it. I have climbed on the burning mountain, and on a cold day I have seen its steam rising from a distance. On the darkest of nights I have literally looked into its white-hot glow. Anyone who gets close enough can feel its warmth. No matter how cold the winter winds, or how deep the snow, the burning mountain melts it all away as a testimony of the burning within.

Early in 1980, I had what could be referred to as a dangerous vein running through my life. I was living in darkness. I was determined never to get married, and as far back as high school I had decided never to bring a child into such a dangerous and contentious world. I was physically wasting away on a crash coarse of alcohol and drug addiction. Several of my close friends took their own lives and many others died from the effects of drug abuse. My own days were numbered. I was living my life in a pit of darkness as dangerous as any coal mine. But more devastating than my perception of marriage or the rearing of children, even worse than the physical destruction of my body, was the loss of my childhood relationship with the Savior. For as a little boy, I knew that God lived. I knew that Jesus was the Christ and I loved my Savior.

My life today is quite different from what it was back in 1980. As a member of the Carmichael Stake Presidency, it has been my good fortune to accompany President Massey and his first counselor, Glen Wahlquist as they visit the homes of departing young men, women, and adult couples, who have received calls to serve full-time missions for the Church. After a prayer with the family, President Massey uses the scriptures to teach the missionaries lessons of service, obedience and love. He always uses President Wahlquist, as a righteous example. He served an honorable mission, came home, married in the temple, and together with his wife raised a house full of missionaries. President Massey might then explain that he and I are converts to the Church and have not yet had the opportunity to serve full-time missions. How grateful we are and what admiration we have for those missionaries who taught us. Our lives are changed, and those missionaries had a lot to do with the blessings that we enjoy today.

After President Massey finishes counseling the soon-to-be set apart missionary, he usually turns to us as counselors and asks if we have anything we want to share. One of us inevitably brings up the fact that a successful mission should never be measured by the number of baptisms a missionary participates in. On many occasions I have shared the fact that the missionaries who taught me the gospel, while I was vacationing in Hawaii, never saw me get baptized. I have often thought of those young men. Each night after meeting with me, they would ask when they could teach me again. My answer was always the same, "Why not tomorrow night?" Every night they came, and every night I kept them past their curfew. By then the buses had stopped running and I could drive them home. That way I could spend more time with them. It felt good to be with them, but at the time I didn't know why.

Years later, I felt a desire to contact my missionaries. I wanted to tell them that I had accepted their challenge. They told me that if I wanted to know if The Church of Jesus Christ of Latter-day Saints was really the restored gospel, or if I wanted to know if The Book of Mormon was really the word of God, written by prophets who lived on this, the American Continent, not to take their word for it, but to pray about the things they taught me. They said I could know for myself, by the power of the Holy Ghost if these things were true. I thought my missionaries might be happy to know that the answer to my prayers was an explosion of sorts. One that blew me literally out of the dark, and into the light. The explosion of my testimony caused a great fire to burn inside me, a fire that is still burning after seventeen years.

I thought my missionaries might like to hear about the day I was standing on a ladder painting a house, shortly after I got back to Colorado from my vacation. At that time in my life, I was playing saxophone in a rock and roll band, but when we weren't traveling around playing music, I subsidized my income by painting houses. That day there was a very real war going on inside my head. My thoughts were consumed by the negative accusations of those who were trying to dissuade me from joining the Church. Almost everyone I knew had something negative to say about "The Mormons." But for some reason, their words never rang true. No matter what I heard them say, I could not forget the feeling I had when I was with the missionaries. I could not forget the love I felt from the family I stayed with in Hawaii. I could not forget the spirit in their home, or the way they were living. I could not forget how clear the answers were that I received, when I prayed and asked. That day standing on a ladder painting a window, amidst the shafts in the whirlwind, the sweet spirit of truth blossomed in the storm. I had followed the prophet Moroni's promise, *"And when ye shall receive these things, I would exhort you that ye would and ask God, the Eternal Father, in the name of Christ, if these things are not true; and if ye shall ask with a sincere heart, with real intent, having faith in Christ, he will manifest the truth of it unto you, by the power of the Holy Ghost." (Moroni 10:4)* I had prayed and asked for myself. I knew the doctrine was true. The Savior's Church had been restored. I knew that Heavenly Father loved us enough to send modern day prophets. I had no doubt. Even though I didn't know a single member of the Church from coast to coast, and not one member of my family or any of my friends were members, I could not deny what my missionaries had taught me. I knew The Book of Mormon was the word of God, translated by the power of God, by a latter day prophet, even Joseph Smith.

I climbed down the ladder, knocked on the front door and asked the woman of the house if I could use her telephone. I took the yellow pages and looked up The Church of Jesus Christ of Latter-day Saints. I called Bishop Wilmer C. Allen and said, "My name is Steve Burrows. I've had all the discussions. How fast can I be baptized?" It must have been quite a shock for him. He was a brand new bishop. I met with him that night for an interview and with the ward mission leader the following day. I was scheduled to be baptized two weeks later. That night I went to our studio for band practice and told the members of my band that I was getting baptized and that they had two weeks to talk me out of it. Our drummer shook his finger at me and said, "I could tell you things about that John Smith that would curl your hair!"

On June 8, 1980 I was baptized by my bishop, a man who held the priesthood of God, even the Melchizedek Priesthood. Oh how I wished my missionaries could have been there. But I knew in my heart that the covenant I was making was between me and Him who had shown me the way. Him, who suffered for my sins, and for the sins of everyone who had ever or would ever come to the Earth. There was a second explosion that occurred in my testimony on August 29, 1981, when I was sealed to Janice May Williamson, in the Salt Lake Temple. Obstetricians have since reported a half-dozen smaller explosions in my testimony, and they are all girls. The testimony that burns within my little celestial family is one that marriage experts claim will never be extinguished.

At five o'clock in the morning on April 6, 1997, the anniversary of the organization of the Church in this dispensation, I was standing in line for general conference. It was cold on Temple Square in Salt Lake City that morning, but there was a warm missionary reunion that happened. Not a huge gathering of return missionaries, but a quiet and emotional reunion. I found Douglass Barton, one of my missionaries. One week later, I found Ron Leatham, my other missionary.

I am thankful to be counted among the Latter-day Saints, who are
"...a chosen generation, a royal priesthood, an holy nation,
a peculiar people..."
Together we can strive to *"...shew forth the praises of him*
who hath called [us] out of darkness [and] into his marvellous light."
(1 Peter 2:9)

Author
Stephen E. Burrows

Stephen E. Burrows joined The Church of Jesus Christ of Latter-day Saints at the age of twenty-five. He is currently serving as a counselor in the Carmichael California Stake. He has served as a bishop, branch president, high counsilor, Melchezidek Priesthood group leader, Scout master, Young Men president, and more.

A native of Aspen, Colorado, he has lived an exciting life of adventure from extreme skiing on 14,000 foot peaks, indoor sky-diving, and rock climbing, to slap-boxing with Muhammad Ali.

He married Janice May Williamson in the Salt Lake Temple. They live in Carmichael, California with their six daughters.

Brother Burrows has been a commercial painter, musician, service station manager, franchise owner, and is currently a certified interpreter for the deaf and deaf/blind. He has interpreted for general conference, and for President Gordon B. Hinkley.

In his spare time he interprets for early morning Seminary, teaches a stake sign language class, is a freelance writer, author and is trying to learn more languages.

Windmill Publishing and Stephen E. Burrows are currently working on other inspirational books. If you have written a story or have a personal experience that you feel would be a benefit for others to read, please send it to:

Windmill Publishing
5740 Windmill Way, Suite 11
Carmichael, CA. 95608
(916) 966-MILL (6455)

Or visit us on the World Wide Web at:
www.windmillpublishing.com